PEACEFUL PERIODS:
HOLISTIC WOMB CARE FOR TEENS

BY CHANTAL BLAKE

Foreword by: Dr. Laurena L. White, MD, MPH, LAc

Copyright © 2023 by Chantal Blake.

All rights reserved. No part of this publication may be reproduced, stored in a retrieval system, or transmitted in any form or by any means, electronic or otherwise, including photocopying, recording, and internet access without prior permission of Chantal Blake.

The content of this book is for informational purposes only and is not intended as a substitute for professional medical advice and/or treatment.

ISBN: 978-1-913478-86-5

Illustrator: Sumaya Asvat
Cover Designer and Formatter: Reyhana Ismail

For inquiries, please visit www.honoredwomb.com

Peaceful Periods: Holistic Womb Care for Teens is approved by Good Gynecology. Good Gynecology is a standard in gynecological medicine that only accepts treatment options that enhance quality of life and well-being in both long and short term with an 80% success rate or higher as acceptable common practice. According to Good Gynecology, the uterus is considered a vital organ important to overall physical and mental health, and pain is not dismissed as normal. The Good Gynecology model of care acknowledges cultural, folk and indigenous women's health practices that predate modern western gynecology encouraging integrative models that work together for the best possible health outcomes.

DEDICATION

In remembrance of our foremothers
who bled without celebration
and cycled without honor.

We honor your wombs,
as we honor our own,
and the wombs that descend from us.

TABLE OF CONTENTS

Foreword	9
A Note to Parents & Guardians: How to Support Your Teen's Peaceful Period Journey	12
Introduction: Your Period is Power	16
Chapter 1: How Will a Better Period Help Me Live My Best Life?	20
Chapter 2: Why Do We Even Have Periods? Ugh!	24
Chapter 3: Isn't It Easier to Just Take a Pill?	29
Chapter 4: Cramps, Constipation, and Crazy Moods: What to Do?	33
Chapter 5: Why Do I Feel So Different Every Week?	44
Chapter 6: Pink, Brown, Watery: Why is My Period Like This?	52
Chapter 7: Slippery, Sticky, Creamy: What's Going on in My Underwear?	60
Chapter 8: Ready to Meet Your Peaceful Period BFFs?	65
Chapter 9: Cravings and Crashes: What am I Supposed to Eat?	77
Chapter 10: Should I Work Out or Chill Out?	87
Chapter 11: How Do I Know When My Period is Coming?	91
Chapter 12: Can Period Power Change the World?	97

Chapter 13: What If I Don't Have a Period?	101
Conclusion	104
Glossary	107
Acknowledgments	115
Dive Deeper	117
Real Talk: When Periods Feel Unbearable	119
Ancient Wisdom for Modern Times, Interview with Acupuncturist Dr. Emily Siy	122
Not Just Hot Air, Interview with Peristeam Hydrotherapist Keli Garza	124
Simple and Sweet, Interview with Homeopath Michelle Pickering	126
Resource Hub	129
Homeopathic Remedy Chart	130
Seasonal Self-Care Reference Chart	132
Emotional Release Technique by Dr. Nicole Monteiro	134
Links and Freebies	136
References	137
Index	139
Author Biography	145

BOOK REVIEWS

"*Peaceful Periods* is a wonderful guide to optimal womb health, wellness, and healing. Chantal does a phenomenal job of preparing teenagers, mothers, parents, and guardians for menarche, the official beginning of a young woman's journey into womanhood. Each chapter delves into the nuanced nature of the physical, mental, and socioemotional aspects of the peaceful period journey. The text is not only informative but also empowering due to her personal account in the introduction. The book is not only relatable but also addresses much of the misinformation and disinformation that most of us received in our 7th-grade health classes. Teenagers who read this book will, as adult women, be more prepared to understand their bodies and ultimately better educated and better equipped to advocate for themselves in a conventional medicine setting that continues to marginalize underserved women."

-Dr. Laurena L. White, MD, MPH, LAc

"This book is like a love letter to young people learning about their menstruation process. It gives a lot of important information in a way that gives space for them to love themselves, their bodies, and the things it goes through to be whole. I love the journal prompts that allow for reflection and exploration. I believe this book would be a beautiful gift between parents and young people where they can learn together and also form a deeper connection with each other. It feels like something to be shared in a sacred way."

-Dr. Emily Siy, DACM, LAc

"*Peaceful Periods: Holistic Womb Care for Teens* by Chantal Blake is a must-read for any young girl navigating her relationship with her body and her period. This book is a comprehensive guide that educates teens on the biology of menstruation and empowers them to embrace their bodies and feel confident in who they are.

"Blake seamlessly weaves together the topics of period positivity, body image, self-esteem, and healthy living, creating a holistic approach to understanding and accepting one's menstrual cycle. She encourages readers to view their periods as a natural and beautiful part of their bodies rather than something to dread or be ashamed of.

"What sets this book apart is Blake's personal experiences with her own period struggles, which make the content relatable and engaging. She shares how her journey to period positivity helped her overcome these challenges. And she shares with readers all of the information and tools she wished she had growing up.

"Overall, *Peaceful Periods* is an empowering and informative read that will leave young women feeling confident and proud of their bodies. It's a must-have for any teen girl's bookshelf and a valuable resource for parents and educators looking to support young girls through this vital stage of womanhood."

-Dr. Nicole Monteiro, Licensed Psychologist

"As a Muslim certified sexual health educator, I highly recommend the book *Peaceful Periods: Holistic Womb Care for Teens* to anyone looking for comprehensive and insightful information on menstrual health. The book offers a holistic approach to understanding the menstrual cycle, covering topics such as anatomy, menstrual hygiene, and emotional well-being during periods.

"What sets this book apart is its focus on truly explaining how and why a woman's body works the way it does when it is in its various phases of reproductive development. *Peaceful Periods* is a welcome addition to an ever-growing field of literature that seeks to shift the narrative around women's reproductive health.

The book is well-researched, easy to read, and offers a much-needed perspective on an often-stigmatized topic. I highly recommend this book to anyone interested in promoting menstrual health and well-being."

-Angelica Lindsey-Ali, Founder of The Village Auntie Institute

"*Peaceful Periods* is a much-needed companion for all teens to learn about their bodies with such approachable and practical information. Chantal has a gift of sharing timeless wisdom with a loving, supportive, and super relatable tone. I especially love the note to parents at the beginning because it supports that idea that "It takes a village." I'm so encouraged and inspired that Chantal wrote this jewel of a book that contains digestible chapters for teens to not only learn about their cycles as a vital sign but also approach some challenges that may come up. I hope this reaches the hands and hearts of all teens as they journey through this rite."

-Kris González, LAc

"I can't wait to buy this book for my daughters and nieces. I can't stop talking about it to all of my friends with daughters, and everyone feels a big sense of relief that someone has finally put a book like this together. How and why girls and women are expected to function without basic information about our menstrual cycles is beyond me. I'm so grateful that *Peaceful Periods: Holistic Womb Care for Teens* has now filled that much-needed gap in girls' education (and the rest of us that never had this info until now and have been sorely missing it!)."

-Keli Garza, Steamy Chick Institute Founder

FOREWORD

MENSTRUAL DYSFUNCTION.

With over 20 years of service and experience in the field of women's health ranging from birth doula to obstetrics/gynecology and reproductive endocrinology/infertility, including acupuncture and Chinese herbal medicine, I am a disruptor. As the clinical director of The Eudaimonia Center, an integrative reproductive medicine and women's health oasis, I lead a team that facilitates the health, wellness, and healing of complex women's health challenges, including but not limited to uterine fibroids, endometriosis, polycystic ovarian syndrome, chronic fatigue syndrome, fibromyalgia, menopausal symptoms, and fertility challenges without the use of unnecessary pharmaceutical drugs (including synthetic hormones and painkillers) and fruitlessly invasive surgical interventions. The root cause and common thread that underlies all these conditions? Menstrual dysfunction. While I know that I haven't seen it all, because of my approach to care, I have seen way more than the average, garden-variety gynecologist.

Nipple hair? Physiologically normal. A treasure trail? Physiologically normal, also. Even body hair, sometimes even in the places we don't want it, serves as a protective barrier and is... physiologically normal, normal, normal. In middle school or junior high, when breasts (or lack thereof) and push-up bras were often the center of attention for girls (and boys alike), general insecurities shifted to other aspects of our bodies. If I could turn back the hand of time, I would overhaul the middle school health education curriculum to include clear and HONEST information about how cisgender female anatomy differs depending on the individual body. Not all vaginas and nipples are the same color but rather different hues and shades in the same way that people of different ethnic backgrounds range in shade and hue.

And vaginas. The scent of a healthy vagina can range from tangy or fermented to coppery or pungent, but never like sweet-smelling flowers, fruit, or perfume (and if yours does, you should be concerned). Healthy vaginas will have a scent; however, they should NOT have an odor. Understand the difference? Many of the products that we use on our bodies and in our vaginas are endocrine (hormone) disruptors that interfere with a healthy pH balance which leads to infections which leads to the addition of more products being introduced into our vaginas and on our skin... and so the cycle begins.

Speaking of cycles, most adult women are at best unclear about the anatomy and physiology of their reproductive systems and associated menstrual cycles, including the ovaries, the fallopian tubes, the uterus, and yes... hormones. We were educated to believe that irregular cycle length and duration, pain, PMS, and even wild variations in the color of our menstrual blood are just part of... being a woman. Not only can these descriptions be daunting, but they can also make being a woman sound like a death sentence at times. Misinformation and disinformation from social media and the conventional medicine disease management system have done considerable damage to the health of adult women and even more damage to our girls and young women.

Into this discord walks Chantal Blake. The physiologically healthy menstrual cycle is a tightly coordinated cycle of stimulatory and inhibitory effects that results in the release of a single mature oocyte from a pool of hundreds of thousands of primordial oocytes. A variety of factors contribute to the regulation of this process, including hormones. The four parameters used to define physiologically healthy/optimal uterine bleeding are: frequency, regularity, duration, and volume. The menstrual cycle is a key indicator of overall health, not just reproductive health, for women of reproductive age. As such, it is of paramount importance that girls and young women understand their bodies and, ultimately, themselves better. In *Peaceful Periods: Holistic Womb Care for Teens*, Chantal Blake begins the re-education process about holistic womb wellness and care with personal anecdotes and continues to provide the reader with integrative approaches to health, wellness, and healing. This book is a revolutionary tool of empowerment especially designed for teenagers, parents, and guardians. Each chapter illuminates womb attunement from a holistic perspective while highlighting how natural, non-pharmaceutical interventions adequately address womb health and wellness concerns while reinforcing the body's innate ability to heal itself.

In a country whose healthcare system falls woefully short of addressing the comprehensive needs of the least of these, namely Black women and girls, this book aims to help parents and guardians partner with their teenage daughters about their period journeys. While presenting some information that confronts the status quo, Chantal creates space for candid and open dialogue in a space that has been previously filled with potentially destructive ideas and concepts. In introducing and re-introducing the reader to an integrative approach to womb wellness, Chantal promotes womb health and overall well-being in ways that are tailored for the reader and easily digestible. Womb care... centered around the individual and her needs, wants, and desires.

-Dr. Laurena L. White, MD, MPH, LAc

A NOTE TO PARENTS & GUARDIANS: HOW TO SUPPORT YOUR TEEN'S PEACEFUL PERIOD JOURNEY

Welcome, Friend!

It is both an honor and a privilege to know that my book is in your hands. It tells me something that I already suspected— you really care for your teen. It also tells me something incredibly hopeful— you want to see a world in which menstruating folks can experience their periods in peace. You don't want the young people in your life to be amongst the 71% of women globally who report period pain or the 20% of young women who miss school because of it.

I'll also assume you don't want the teens in your life to be among the 1.5 million women between the ages of 15-19 who take synthetic birth control for non-contraceptive reasons. If you suspect that there are natural and holistic ways to address the common complaints of cramps, PMS, hormonal acne, heavy bleeding, menstrual irregularity, etc.- then you are in the right place.

When I first shared this manuscript with parents of teenagers, they raved about how informative the contents of this book were. Even as adults, they learned a lot. But many asked a really important question: How can teens do this work on their own?

I believe that young people are incredibly resourceful and intelligent. There is so much they can do on their own once they've discovered their motivations. However, here are a few ways that you can be a partner in their peaceful period journey.

1. Please be open. In this book, you will come across information about periods that seems unfamiliar and surprising. As a former health care professional myself, I have been frustrated and shocked about how lacking

my period education was before adulthood. The ideas presented here may challenge and confront you. I ask that you give yourself time to listen to the ideas, interrogate any resistance you feel arising, and give space to consider a new perspective or point of view.

2. Protect the primary fuel sources: food and rest. Nutrition is a critical contributor to hormonal balance. The diets we may have adopted for convenience, modernity, or efficiency don't necessarily meet our older and wiser biology. I invite you to examine your food access and choices. If you eat animal products, please note that the quality of what you consume significantly impacts your health. Factory-farmed animals are exposed to grossly different diets, conditions, and experiences than pasture-fed, free-range animals. I implore you, for the sake of your family's health and the health of our planet, to seek out the highest quality animal foods that you can afford and source them from as close to home as possible. If you can only afford conventionally-raised animal products, I invite you to lean on your vegetarian allies like eggs, cheese, legumes, and beans as core ingredients in your family's meal plans. Note that when preparing dried beans, legumes, and grains, soaking them overnight and/or fermenting them improves digestibility and nutrient assimilation.

3. Phase out chemicals. Swap conventional cleaning products and skin and hair care products for non-toxic alternatives. Endocrine-disrupting chemicals abound in scented household cleaners and personal care products. You can start by transitioning to unscented, color-free household products such as detergents, dishwashing liquids, surface cleaners, soaps, shampoos, lotions, etc. Alternatively, baking soda and white vinegar can be great substitutes. When thinking of adding a scent to your cleaners, keep in mind that the high potency of essential oils can also challenge hormonal balance and upset our natural microbiome. However, vinegar infused with citrus peels or fragrant herbs and hydrosols carry the plant properties we love without overwhelming our bodies.

4. Minimize plastic content. Following the previous point, endocrine-disrupting chemicals can transfer from plastic water bottles and food storage containers into our bodies. This is a great time to move away from bottled drinking water in favor of filtered water or naturally sourced water. If water is not a regularly consumed beverage in your home, you can add fresh herbs, lemon slices, or fruits to make it more appealing.

5. Make space for protected rest. Rest is becoming a scarce commodity for youth and adults alike. There seems to be a competition to determine the minimum amount of sleep we need to function well. However, both rest quantity and quality are being disrupted by light pollution, after-hours screen use, and overstimulating lives that don't have an unwinding routine at the end of the day. By setting boundaries around screen use and bright lights just before bedtime, we can help our teens have deep, restorative rest that balances and recharges them to face a new day. Providing your teen with blue light blocking screen protectors or glasses can help limit the stimulating effect of screen use after hours. Also, modeling time boundaries that encourage winding down at the end of the day can help the entire family enjoy nourishing rest.

6. Prioritize period care. Many of us were not taught that menstruation is very different from any other time of the month. The overall implication is: yes, you are bleeding, but put a pad on, pop some pain pills, and get on with the show, whether that is school, work, chores, or other responsibilities. One cause that I passionately advocate for is to honor the period through self-care. How can you cultivate space for your teen to have some downtime when they bleed? Can they take a day off from school? Have a break from house chores? Be excused from extracurricular activities? In a world that belittles menstruation, it is a revolutionary act to resist the status quo. We dishonor the tremendous work of our wombs every month when we push ourselves instead of resting.

7. Invite self-expression. Perhaps you've been following me well on the previous points and are wondering: what does this have to do with periods? Honestly, the answer is a lot. Repressed emotions and unexpressed needs often reveal themselves in period patterns. If you ever considered why a grieving widow might experience a delayed period or an anxious bride might experience an early bleed, these clues point to the heart-womb connection. In Traditional Chinese Medicine teachings, there is a channel that connects the heart and womb. In physiology, we can observe how tension in the jaw or lack of expression from the throat results in pelvic floor tension signaling a lack of safety, acceptance, and ability to fully exist as you are. Pelvic tension contributes to period pain, as well as other challenging conditions like pelvic pain, vaginismus, blood stagnation, etc. How can you create space for the fluid expression of thoughts, feelings, and ideas in your household? How can you also follow through with space for movement like play, dance, and exercise, which unwind tension held in the pelvic floor?

8. Period product availability. In this book, I advocate for more sustainable period product choices. They not only positively impact our hormonal health but also reduce pollution waste. This might be a challenge for you. Investing in plastic-free, non-toxic disposal pads is worthwhile but not always affordable. Similarly, you might need time to adjust psychologically to the use of reusable cloth pads and period panties, especially if you've grown accustomed to the use of disposables. Or perhaps, you might need some space to work out new laundry habits. Please get curious with your teen about options that make sense for you and your family.

9. I'd like you to take the time to read this book for yourself too. You don't necessarily have to read it with your teen, but if you menstruate, I promise that there are practices and advice here that will serve you. Even if you're closer to menopause than menarche, the pillars of hormonal balance are the same for you and your teen— stable blood sugar, well-managed stress, healthy elimination, and detoxification. Most of these practices will even serve you well into your elder years, so please be curious, read along, and let me know your thoughts.

You can email me at chantal@honoredwomb.com

INTRODUCTION: YOUR PERIOD IS POWER

Welcome, Love!

I'm so glad you're here. I know it isn't always easy to talk about periods. Sometimes we don't know who to talk to or who wants to hear what we have to say. I'm hoping by reading this book, you'll understand your body and know you're not alone in your experience. Whether it's cramps, brown spotting, or smelly mucus in your underwear, you'll better understand why it's happening and what you can do about it. And maybe, when you realize that something you thought was strange is really quite common, you might not feel so shy to talk about periods.

I didn't talk about my period very much when I was a teenager. I was the youngest in my circle of friends and the last to start my period. Everyone around me talked about cramps and pads, and I was just waiting for my turn to join the conversation. When I did start my period, it was a bit of a blur. I don't remember where I was or what I was doing. I just remember being 13 and going to school the next day, feeling like I was finally a part of 'the club.' I could now complain about periods too with my friends. It felt like I belonged with all the others, but by the age of 15, I was over it.

Vivid in my memory is a laidback lesson at the end of my school day. It was my junior year in high school, and we were watching the movie Waiting for Godot. Much like the book, it's a slow story that involves a lot of waiting. I slouched in my seat with my legs crossed, resting my head on my hand. When the bell rang, I was so ready to go home and leaped up to leave. That's when a classmate pulled me aside. My pale blue dress had a bright red stain, and it was spreading. Thankfully, I had a sweater to wrap around my waist, but I still felt so embarrassed. I had a mile-long walk to the bus stop and kept wiping my hand over my sweater every few minutes to make sure I hadn't leaked through.

Stains and pains soon became a consistent part of my period life. Strangely though, it's something that my friends and I bonded over. How much we hated our periods and cramps became some kind of an inner club that we all belonged to. It took me many years to realize that I could make choices to influence my period. We saw ourselves as victims of our bodies, but really, we were looking at it all in the wrong way.

By the time I was 17 years old, I was living on campus at a college in Pennsylvania. It was my first time living away from home. I felt lucky that my period wouldn't come every month, but when it did, it was always memorable. I would be doubled over in my top bunk bed, laying alone and waiting for pain medicine to give relief. I didn't know that there was something else I could do other than suffer. I didn't know that certain foods and teas could help me just as much, if not more, than a pill. Even worse, I didn't know how much my poor eating and sleeping habits contributed to my period drama.

My first pain-free period wasn't until my sophomore year of college. I moved off campus to live in a three-story home with five friends. We were exploring new ideas and ways of living. Terms like "straight edge," "anarchist," and "conscious" were being thrown around as we all explored our identities, labels, and how we fit into the world around us. At some point, many of my closest friends were vegan and vegetarian— some in response to the poor treatment of factory-farmed animals, some for spiritual reasons, and others for overall health and wellness. I found their perspectives intriguing and enjoyed a few meat-free meals with them.

My first vegetarian meal was a total failure. In my college's dining hall, there were several dining choices. A salad bar filled with a colorful assortment of toppings and veggies, a hot food bar filled with American dishes that were foreign to my Caribbean taste buds, a waffle and omelet station for all-day breakfast dining, and a pasta stand stationed by a jovial chef named James from Philly. I ate pasta with ground beef, tomato sauce, and a sprinkling of onions and bell peppers almost every night. It was the most familiar food I could find.

One particular day, I asked James to skip the beef and give me veggies instead. My college dorm neighbor was a passionate environmental activist and vegan. Images of sick and caged animals from the PETA handouts she gave me when we first met haunted me. I thought it only fair to give a meat-free life a chance. But, I found myself still hungry after a whole plate of pasta and quickly concluded that this way of eating wouldn't work for me. Once I started eating off-campus, I discovered new cuisines and their tastier vegetarian alternatives, like Mexican bean bowls, Chana Masala, vegan Pad Thai, and Hummus. Life without meat was starting to feel possible.

Moving off-campus meant I also had to buy groceries, so I had the opportunity to experiment with new foods, like canned black beans, fresh kale, and organic milk. I soon discovered that I felt more energized after meals which meant I could study after dinner, as opposed to feeling heavy and drowsy. I also noticed that I was sleeping less and waking up feeling lighter in the morning and ready for the day. I experienced fewer stomach aches and became sick less often too. But what really sold me on this new way of eating was how easy my period became.

My week of heavy bleeding shortened to just a few days. My cramping pain disappeared, and I had way more energy than before. My mind was blown. How come no one told me that what I eat impacts my period? Why didn't I know that heavy bleeding wasn't a necessary part of my month? I felt like valuable information I was mature enough to understand was kept from me. Information that would have given me the power to make better choices for myself.

Now, I'm not saying that the answer to your period problems is to become vegetarian (though most teens would benefit from more veggies in their diets for sure!), but I do want you to know that you are not powerless regarding your period. You can consciously make choices about how to feed, move, and rest in a way that will impact your period. I want you to know the simple science about how your body works so you can understand and choose how you want to experience your body. You can deal with your period when it comes, or you can have a plan and know exactly what to do to have peaceful periods every single month.

The content you'll learn in this book is what I teach women and teenagers through courses, workshops, and social media. It would have been really helpful to me if I had known this when I was your age. I would have felt so empowered to know that my pesky period symptoms were just my body's way of communicating with me. Being the problem-solver I am, it would have been like a science project to change my lifestyle and see how my period responds. While I can't turn back time, it brings me a lot of joy and hope to teach teens like you. I look forward to hearing how this book impacted you and receiving your feedback. If you're on Instagram, tag me at @honoredwomb. On all platforms, you can use the hashtag

#peacefulperiodsbook to share pics of you reading this book or applying something you learned from it.

Here's a quick orientation- I'm assuming you've already gone through puberty and have a basic sense of body parts like vulva, vagina, uterus, and ovaries. I'll be talking about these body parts often, so here's a quick refresher, just in case you forgot.

To menstruate, some key body parts are needed, namely a uterus or womb, ovaries, uterine tubes (also known as Fallopian tubes), and a vaginal canal. These interior parts are critical to reproduction and menstruation.

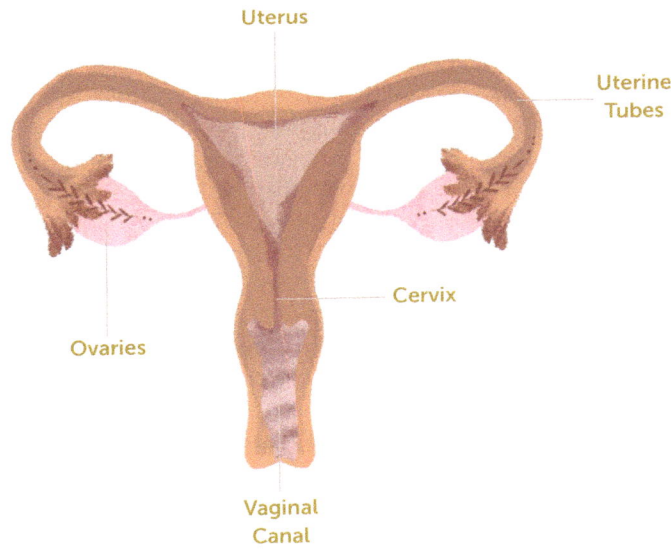

Externally, our menstrual flow exits from our vaginal opening, which is beneath the clitoris and urethra and above the perineum and anus. See Chapter 7 for more details.

The content of this book revolves around the menstrual cycle, and the tone of my writing is directed to readers who have periods. Even if you don't have a period, I believe this book will help you better understand how to love and care for someone who does. I thank you for picking this book up and pray that it benefits you and those you love.

CHAPTER 1:
HOW WILL A BETTER PERIOD HELP ME LIVE MY BEST LIFE?

Have you ever imagined your dream life? About ten years from now, what would you like to do? With whom? And where? Can you see yourself as a professional gamer in Tokyo, a groundbreaking architect in Dubai, or a homesteading mom in San Diego? Regardless of how big and bold your goals are, I have a question for you: what does your dream life feel like when you're on your period? Would your period get in the way, or can you imagine your period helping you live your very best life?

Some see their period as disruptive. They feel like their period arrives unannounced, ready to ruin their day. If they have cramps, they might pop some painkillers and carry on with their plans as if nothing is happening. If they're bleeding heavily, they might wear both a tampon and a pad for fear of bleeding through their clothes. But what if we see the period as helping us achieve what we want in life, not disrupting it?

Regardless of what you'll do as an adult, you'll likely spend some time studying, planning, working, creating, speaking, organizing, reflecting, and analyzing. All of those tasks are critical to most types of work. Most people don't think too much about when exactly to do which task, but timing or syncing your tasks to how your body and brain focus shifts every month is your secret sauce. There are times when your ability to do each work task is exponentially better or easier than doing the same task at another time in the month. Let me explain.

THE FULL CYCLE

If I told you exactly when your brain's creativity and ability to learn and store new information peaks every month, would you schedule your study time, brainstorming sessions, and team meetings at that time? Or, if you knew that at a specific timeframe, all of your lovely hormones heighten your ability to communicate, give you glowing skin, and improve your social skills, how would you use that opportunity? How about a particular phase in your menstrual cycle when your brain requires deep, focused work and is stellar at organizing, completing tasks, and setting limits with people so that you can complete your projects and tasks? And what if I told you that your body has a built-in biological "time-out" when it needs to rest, recharge, and rebuild so that you can reemerge to creatively and energetically live your best life all over again every month?

From period to period, your body moves to nature's rhythm. If you want to grow anything, you must be willing to go through the phases of preparing, growing, harvesting, and resting. If you want to accomplish a goal, there is similarly a cycle of planning, working, evaluating, and reflecting. Your menstrual cycle is no different. Like every miracle of nature, there is a season for everything. We find balance in knowing how and when to step up, switch up, and slow down the tempo of our lives.

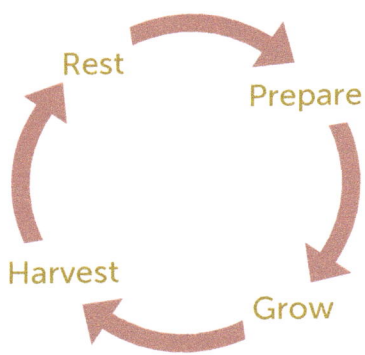

Instead of becoming irritable or moody the week before your period, frustrated by bloating, and finding yourself 'hangry' and ready to blow up at someone, imagine knowing what exactly you need to eat, what to focus on, and how to care for yourself, so your premenstrual symptoms are minimal or non-existent. You open your period journal or tracking calendar and know exactly which foods to pick for lunch at school or in a cafe with your friends because you know some foods will help your hormones more than others right now.

How would it feel to know when to expect your period so you make sure your calendar is cleared and you wrap up all of your to-do list items beforehand? Your projects are done, you let your coach know you won't be training, and your parents give you a break from chores, so you can slow down when you're on your period. When you feel a craving, you understand what your body needs and know how to support yourself with food.

READY TO CHOOSE PEACE?

Imagine feeling empowered to know your choices can impact your experiences and symptoms in real time. You know exactly how to evaluate every period and use it as a map to stay on course and make changes to improve your next period. I don't want you to bleed your life away for 7-10 days every month or longer. I want you to have a moderate four-day flow without clots, cramps, or pain once every 28-30 days. I want you to glide through the PMS jungle unscathed because you know how to maneuver through the shifts your body is going through without getting caught in 'moody' traps or 'bloating' obstacles.

Having a peaceful period is not a myth or joke. It's actually the natural result of a well-balanced system. When your body feels adequately supported in all realms- nutrition, activity, rest, self-care, and stress management, you can live in the flow of your monthly rhythm. By learning how to live in tune with your menstrual cycle now, you'll be able to have a healthy relationship with food, your body image, self-esteem, and meaningful relationships with others. You don't have to clean up the damage of an emotional wreck every month, like canceling plans with your BFF at the last minute or raging at a younger sibling. You'll have the tools to check in with yourself and know what you need for support according to where you're at in your menstrual cycle and what your body needs.

What you'll learn in this book will help you show up authentically in all kinds of relationships in your life right now as well as later in life. Balanced hormones will support you in feeling deeply bonded and connected with those you love. You'll know the best time to plan trips, dates, or new experiences. If you plan to have a family one day, you'll know exactly when you're fertile, so you can plan to achieve or avoid pregnancy. In your career, you'll be able to schedule work activities, team projects, and breaks in ways that allow you to use all of your period gifts when they shine brightest. And as a parent, you can show your children how to live a balanced life by modeling self-care and healthy boundaries with others. They will learn from watching you that a menstruating body is constantly changing, and no one should expect us to feel, move, and perform the same way every day.

Your period is not here to ruin your life but rather to connect you to life. You get to experience the strengths of your mind, body, and heart in different ways throughout the month.

So let's learn how to get rid of period pain and bring more period power into your life, shall we?

CHAPTER RECAP:

- Periods aren't meant to throw our lives off course every month.
- A peaceful period can be achieved when we better understand how to give our body what it needs.
- Scheduling your plans and activities around your period can help you experience fewer challenges.

Journal Prompt:

Do you remember your first period?

Where were you and what were you doing?

How did you feel?

CHAPTER 2:
WHY DO WE EVEN HAVE PERIODS? UGH!

Have you ever wondered what your life would be like without your period? No pads? No bleeding? Just floating through each month the same way you did before puberty. I remember having painful cramps, heavy bleeding, and irregular periods as a teenager. I was that friend who never knew when her period was coming and found it quite cool that it didn't come every month. I didn't know every period is a personal report card to tell us how our body is doing. I just thought fewer periods meant fewer problems for me.

Periods are so important that some doctors call it our fifth vital sign. Much like other vital signs— body temperature, blood pressure, heart rate, and breathing rate— your period holds essential data about your health and hormones. Unfortunately, the conversation about periods on most doctors' visits is limited to just "When was your last period?" and not much more. But when you get into the nitty-gritty details like the color of your flow, the number of days you bleed, the consistency of your flow, and what symptoms you experience before and during your period, you decode the language of your body, and it all begins to make sense.

Care providers that can help you deeply understand what your period is trying to communicate include acupuncturists, functional medicine practitioners, naturopaths, Ayurvedic practitioners, and peristeam hydrotherapists. Many of these care providers can give you deeper insight into your period health by understanding your symptoms and making observations.

BACK TO BASICS

Just the fact that you have a period means that your body believes it is mature and healthy enough to begin ovulation. Ovulation is the release of a mature egg. Starting your period doesn't mean you should start having babies. But it does mean that your body wants to start practicing the monthly sequence of events that will help you have a healthy baby in the future. Just like seeds in nature, you have way more eggs than you'll ever need to have a family.

You're born with over a million immature egg follicles in your ovaries. What I find cool about this is your biological mother carried you as an immature egg while still in the womb or uterus of your grandmother. So, even if you've never met your maternal grandmother, at some point in time, you were nourished in her body, by her blood, before you even took your first breath.

This also means any potential children you may have are already inside you. Little seeds of possibilities that we won't know until the future. You had your highest number of eggs when you were a 20-week-old fetus in your mother's womb. They began decreasing soon after and continue to release as you age. By your first period, you only have about half a million eggs, and this number is reduced with every menstrual cycle. The eggs are never replaced. Ovulating or releasing eggs every month is not just for pregnancy preparation. It also helps your body become an expert at a vital conversation using the language of hormones.

HORMONE KNOW-HOW

Hormones are the chemical messengers in your body that give your organs their marching orders. Your endocrine system is the motherboard that dictates when and how hormones get released to different parts of your body. The entire process of menstruating (that simply means period bleeding) and ovulation (egg release) jumpstarts crucial hormones that impact so much more than your periods and pregnancy.

Hormones triggered by the process of ovulation, as well as what follows it, can impact your:

- energy levels
- how fast your body uses energy from the foods you eat
- the quality of your hair and skin
- which parts of your brain to optimize
- how your body gains weight
- what foods you crave
- and much more

While terms like "hormonal" are often associated with having mood swings or emotional instability, hormones are powerful and can be our superpowers every day, week, and month of our lives.

To understand these superpowers, let me first introduce you to some of our key hormones.

Estrogen is the life of the party.

Estrogen gets the party started! As your immature egg or follicle grows to become a mature egg, it makes estrogen which tells your uterus to start preparing a safe landing place for the egg. The egg is pushed out of your ovary and swept into one of your uterine tubes to wait for fertilization. It then works its way down to your uterus. The safe landing pad is created by thickening your uterus' inner lining, which is where a fertilized egg would need to implant to grow a baby. If fertilization doesn't happen, the egg will get reabsorbed into your body or exit with your next period.

Estrogen is also responsible for growing other parts of your body, like your breasts, hips, and butt. Those cushy parts tell your body you are safe and well-fed, so you can help protect, feed, and nurture a growing baby in the future. Estrogen is also a little risky. It helps you try new things and feel fearless, which can be great when you need to tackle an important task like public speaking, a job interview, or having heart-to-heart conversations with others.

Progesterone is your inner chill chick.

Progesterone always seems cool, calm, and collected. It knows how to roll with changing circumstances and isn't easily stressed out or anxious. Even though estrogen makes your uterine lining grow, progesterone keeps that lining in place until your body gets the memo that you're not pregnant. To start your period, progesterone levels drop to trigger the release of your uterine lining, which flows out in your menstrual blood. While losing lining might sound painful, it really shouldn't be. Cramps are not a necessary part of life; I'll explain why later. Blood vessels in your uterus are like faucet pipes that open when it's time to flush out everything that you no longer need. We often think of blood as indicating an injury or damage, but period blood is unique. This blood is the liquid that nourishes your uterine lining, cleanses and heals your vaginal tissues, and transports materials the uterus wants to release.

Follicle Stimulating Hormone (FSH) is like a commander.

On the first day of your period, your brain starts to produce Follicle Stimulating Hormone to get another egg growing for next month's ovulation. Your body wastes no time with egg production, so every month FSH recruits 10-15 follicles (little fluid-filled sacs containing premature eggs) to start growing. Every month, your ovary is growing these follicles, though only one (two at the most) is likely to be released.

Luteinizing Hormone (LH) is like the eject button.
Luteinizing Hormone pushes the most mature egg out of your ovary. I like to imagine that little egg finally in flight like a pilot with only a parachute to guide its descent. Your eggs don't have anything similar to a parachute, but the little balloon sac your egg leaves behind goes through a major change. It turns into a tiny, temporary, yellow organ called the corpus luteum. This little organ is the gland that makes most of our progesterone.

Testosterone is a go-getter.
Testosterone is another key player in your hormonal band. It is a very social hormone that motivates you to connect with others. Most females don't make much of it, but it helps us become more socially engaged and physically strong right before ovulation.

All hormones rise and fall in response to cues and messages sent between your organs and other hormonal levels. When your body is well-supported, all of these messages can be sent, and things can happen harmoniously. But when your body feels stressed because of skipped meals, lots of pressure to perform, hard situations, or habitually staying up way too late, your hormones can get out of whack. All of the above creates a stress signal in your body that can tell your ovaries to stop egg production. Ovulation is the conductor of this amazing hormonal symphony, and the show can't go on without it.

Back to our question: *Why do we have periods?*

In short, our periods tell us we are fertile or that we can create life. This is a huge sign of health in the female body. When our period is healthy, we're healthy. And when it's not, we're not.

CHAPTER RECAP:
- Your period is like a monthly health check. It tells you how well your hormones are working together to release an egg or ovulate every month.
- Having a monthly period is how the body prepares to reproduce one day.
- Each of the hormones that support your period show up at different times of the month, like a theatrical play.

Journal Prompt:

Complete the chart below:

What I Like About Periods	
What I Don't Like About Periods	
What I Would Change About Periods	

CHAPTER 3:
ISN'T IT EASIER TO JUST TAKE A PILL?

If you've already talked to a doctor about period problems like heavy bleeding, intense cramps, or hormonal acne, you've most likely been offered one of two options: pain medication or birth control. The type of pain medication typically recommended for period pain or dysmenorrhea is NSAIDs (non-steroidal, anti-inflammatory drugs). In function, they reduce pain, fever, and inflammation by reducing prostaglandin production. Prostaglandins are hormone-like substances made by fats, which tell your tissues how to respond to inflammation. In the short-term, NSAIDs can be effective for many types of period pain, but long-term use comes with challenging consequences.

Mixed Messages

Pain medication might make some people feel unstoppable. With just a little pill, there is no slowing down or opting out of the activities they really want to do. However, pain is an important message the body sends us, indicating something is not quite right. Period pain, unfortunately, is a very normalized type of pain. We are told that we just have to "stick it out" or "deal with it". And if we can't, "pop a pain pill and quit complaining". But ignoring pain doesn't make it go away, and taking pain medication comes with costs.

Long-term use of NSAIDs like aspirin, ibuprofen, or naproxen can increase your risk for high blood pressure and heart attacks; bloating; stomach ulcers, pain, and bleeding; and kidney problems. Because NSAIDs reduce prostaglandin production, some women report having delayed ovulation or periods without ovulation when using them. Before pain becomes unbearable, here are a few early interventions:

Rest

Slow down your activities, even if that means asking for a day off from school or work. Period pain, in some cases, can be almost as painful as a heart attack. We wouldn't expect someone with a heart attack to study, work, drive, or function as they normally do, so why isn't period pain taken as seriously?

Warm up
Applying a hot water bottle or heating pad to your abdomen can increase blood flow to your womb and sometimes offer relief.

Herbal tea
Herbs like ginger, turmeric, and chamomile have muscle-relaxing and anti-inflammatory properties that can reduce the actual cause of the pain you feel and increase circulation in your body.

Seek help
If pain is a recurring part of your monthly period, something needs to change. In Chapter 4, you'll learn more about period habits, practices, and food choices that can help you minimize period pain for good. You can also find supportive allies in medical practitioners that can help you understand why you're experiencing pain and come up with a comprehensive plan to prevent it for good.

The other pill often offered to teens with difficult periods is birth control. Birth control pills are a form of contraception or pregnancy prevention designed for women. In some places and cultures, women have very little say over their bodies. They may be forced to have children, even when they don't want to or they physically should not. In cases such as these, being able to privately prevent pregnancy can be an opportunity to avoid unwanted children or dangerous pregnancies. This same pill used to avoid pregnancy is commonly prescribed for otherwise treatable period problems. By artificially shutting off ovulation, women are promised temporary relief from some of the hormonal challenges they face, as well as related symptoms like acne, cramps, and heavy bleeding. This 'quick-fix' promise can seem very attractive, but let's explore this further.

By taking daily doses of artificial hormones, the body no longer thinks it needs to ovulate. To feel like your body still has a period, birth control companies mix in placebo (non-acting) pills— creating a withdrawal bleed that may resemble a period but isn't really a period because ovulation has been disrupted.

Stopping ovulation is like telling your hormones: "Quiet! Stop sending me messages and warnings!" This might feel like exactly what you want to say to your body at times, but when we stop getting 'alert' messages, we don't know how to fix the underlying problem. We simply bury it and become further and further from any solution. Birth control pills come with their troubles too—like mood instability, bloating, nausea, weight gain, spotting, skin problems, and blood clots in the legs or lungs (which can be deadly). In the long-term, these side effects can become diabetes, weight gain, yeast infections, risk of cancer, risk of stroke, nutrient depletion, gallstones, deep vein blood clots, shrinking of your pituitary gland and ovaries, and much more.

If you're currently on birth control, you might wonder if you should continue or not. This decision needs to be made with wisdom and support. Regardless of your choice, know that supporting the health of your hormones is always the right choice. What you have in your hands are the tools to have a healthier period once and for all. You can know your body and understand how to feel your very best in it. You don't need to feel like your body is broken, angry, or out to get you. Your body is your friend trying its best to get your attention.

Of course, taking a pill is much easier than trying to understand and respond to what your body needs. But I don't want you to give your period power to a profitable industry that tells you all you need is a pill to improve your life. Spoiler alert: the folks my age who've been regularly taking pain medication and birth control since they were your age aren't having the time of their lives. Long-term use of pain medication increases your risk of heart attacks, kidney damage, and stomach ulcers. Birth control makes young women more prone to depression and more likely to experience diseases, including autoimmunity, cardiac and thyroid conditions, cancer, infections, hair loss, blood clots, and fatigue. Some even have difficulty having a baby later in life because their body has relied so long on artificial hormones instead of producing its own.

Some menstrual conditions can be especially challenging for teens, and I want you to be aware of them and understand how you can be supported. Read more in *Real Talk: When Periods Feel Unbearable* on page 119.

If at any point you feel like your period pain and/or bleeding becomes unbearable, please seek out support from a care provider that has more to offer you than pharmaceuticals and is committed to helping you uncover the root of your experience, not just manage your symptoms.

CHAPTER RECAP:

- Many teens are offered pain medicine or birth control to treat difficult period symptoms.
- Long-term use of both NSAIDs and birth control can negatively impact our health.
- There are period care practices that can help relieve period pain and discomfort.

Journal Prompt:
If your doctor offered you birth control to manage period discomfort, how would you respond? What questions would you ask before making a decision?

CHAPTER 4:
CRAMPS, CONSTIPATION, AND CRAZY MOODS: WHAT TO DO?

Do you ever feel angry at your body? Like, "What are you doing and why?" Sometimes our body seems to mess things up for us. On top of bleeding, you feel cramping pain. Before your period, your breasts are sore, you're constipated, or you're about to snap on everyone. You don't want to feel this way, but you do, and you can't seem to help it, stop it, or make it go away. What to do?

First, I want you to think a little differently about your body. Your brain, blood, muscles, organs, and bones are all intelligently designed. They have been working together as a team to make sure you eat, breathe, rest, stay safe, and stay alive. Every 'symptom' you experience is an important chat message. And when you ignore those messages, the notifications add up. The sender gets agitated and starts WRITING IN ALL CAPS. Maybe even calling you non-stop or worse, giving up and ghosting you. Every message from your body is information. Information telling you what you need at your most basic biological level; for example, rest, food, warmth, and care.

I promise you: when you make a habit of listening to your body's messages and responding to them, your body will start to feel like a safe and peaceful spacesuit with which you may navigate this thing called life. You'll be able to handle stressors and changes without having meltdowns and breakdowns. You'll be resilient, surfing the waves of life, and not struggling to stay afloat with the waves crashing overhead.

So, here's the action plan:

IN-THE-MOMENT RELIEF

One of the greatest gifts of menstruating is the undeniable, attention-getting tug that says, "Hey, friend. Something's happening here." You have a choice when your period knocks. You can say, "Go away! Not now!" Take a few painkillers and get on with your day. Or, you can open the door, greet your friend, and say, "Come on in. I'm glad you're here. I've been expecting you. What can I do for you?" Put on a pot of hot water, pour a cup of tea, and sit with your friend. Take time to hear, listen, and be with your friend.

When we invite our period in, instead of slamming the door in its face, we honor our period as a welcomed part of our life. And when we make a habit of listening, our period won't need to shout, kick, or scream to get our attention. Instead, our period can tug, nudge, or whisper, knowing it won't be ignored, shut out, or suppressed. We care for our period by ultimately caring for ourselves. We make space, get cozy, and find ways to slow down. This could be a great time to put on comfy clothes and watch movies in bed with your parent, sibling, or bestie. Or, if you're feeling more introspective, you can grab a journal to jot down your thoughts, make art, or write poetry. Don't demand that you push through and carry on if you don't have to.

Your period is a 'built-in' time of rest intended to remind you that your bleeding is a blessing. This is not blood from injury or harm but the blood of life itself. How does that sound to you? The blood that flows from your womb is the continuous river that has kept humanity alive since the beginning of existence. Your mother, grandmother, and so on had a monthly bleed, just like you, and this is how you're here today. Some ancient cultures even worshiped menstrual blood because they saw it as sacred and believed women were closer to the spiritual world during their monthly bleed. There are communities that would gather around to hear women's dreams on their periods, looking for guidance and wisdom.

Despite these beautiful ideas about menstruation, having a period doesn't always feel holy and special. Sometimes it sucks. Cramping, diarrhea, and nausea don't feel very sanctified at all. However, these symptoms can be remedied, and here are five Peaceful Period Practices to help you do just that.

PEACEFUL PERIOD PRACTICES

1. Nourishing Food

Starving yourself is never a good idea, especially during your period. Your brilliant body is working hard to do all the things– maturing an egg, growing uterine lining, holding and then shedding that lining, and plenty of other changes to prime your body for possible fertilization and reproduction. You have an increased need for calories and nutrients at this time, so skipping a meal is not the move to make.

2. Warmth
When we feel cold or have cold foods, our blood vessels shrink and move less blood. To help our period flow well, we can use warmth to help our menstrual blood flow with less clotting and cramping. You can add warmth to your womb by laying with a hot water bottle or heating pad, wearing a cozy sweater, sipping herbal tea, or having soups and stews. Warmth allows your blood to flow with ease. Sluggish blood flow can thicken and become brown or clotted, which your uterus may try to help eliminate by cramping or squeezing to help clear things out.

3. Rest
Laying down can do wonders for slowing down a heavy flow. Gravity is always active and adds pressure to your already heavier uterus. Engorged with blood volume and a thickened lining, you are carrying a heavier load - literally. Help your body by lying down and putting your feet up for a bit. After a delicious warm meal, a restful nap can be just what you need to lighten your pain and ease your discomfort.

4. Relaxation
One mineral we often use during our menstrual cycle is magnesium. Ever craved chocolate before or during your period? Well, raw chocolate (cacao) is an excellent source of magnesium and may be the reason your body is trying to get some. You might grab milk chocolate to calm that craving, but it won't give you as much magnesium as dark chocolate. Look for chocolate bars that say 60% cocoa or higher to help your uterine muscles relax. If there's no chocolate handy, try almonds, hazelnuts, avocados, or leafy greens for the same effect. An Epsom salt foot bath or full body bath can also give you a dose of magnesium to soothe sore muscles, uterine cramping, and breast tenderness.

5. Unplug
By design, our uterus sheds its lining by opening our uterine arteries to flush out its mucus layer with fresh blood. This blood is intended to flow freely from our vaginas. If we are blocking that downward flow with tampons or moving our bodies in ways that back up our flow (like handstands and other inverted positions where your hips are above your head), we might notice more cramping in an effort to restore that downward blood flow. As for menstrual cups or discs that collect period blood inside of the vagina, some notice more cramping while using them, and others don't. So, see what works best for you.

Even with these Peaceful Period Care Practices, you might need some support for immediate relief, and this is where homeopathic remedies can be helpful. Homeopathic remedies are prepared as small sweet pellets that easily dissolve in your mouth. If you can't find homeopathic remedies at your local health food store or supplied by your practitioner, they can be ordered online from a homeopathic pharmacy. The remedies' names may sound as cryptic as a Harry Potter spell, but most are named after the plant, mineral, or material they are sourced from.

The remedies are diluted so significantly that almost no detectable amount of the source ingredient is left, so side effects are highly unlikely. However, homeopathy can produce subtle yet potent shifts in your symptoms, even when used as first aid. Learn more about homeopathy in the Dive Deeper section's *"Simple and Sweet, Interview with Homeopath Michelle Pickering"* on page 126.

PRE-PERIOD ACTION PLAN:

Do you feel like your period is coming soon, and you're bracing for the worst? No need! Let's get into action. First, we put a hold on all kinds of fried foods ASAP (as soon as possible). Why? Because the type of fats we eat influences our prostaglandin levels. Prostaglandins are messengers made from fats that tell our tissues how to respond to inflammation. Some prostaglandins tell our uterus to relax, while others tell it to squeeze. If you want more uterus-relaxing messengers, you need more calming fats in your diet, like olive oil, coconut oil, grass-fed butter or ghee, avocados, and nuts. Most fried and packaged foods are cooked with the kinds of oils that our uterus does not love— vegetable oil, canola oil, sunflower oil, cottonseed oil, and the like. If we can pause the chips, fried foods, and packaged snacks, we can bring more calming messengers into the body.

Next, it's time to level up your self-care with Womb Wellness Practices.

1. Womb Steaming

By preparing a warm pot of herbal tea for an in-home pelvic sauna, we can increase circulation to our womb, so it's not working hard to squeeze out clots or thick dark blood. Instead, the added warmth will encourage a healthy start to your monthly flow with a bright red color and steady medium flow. This practice might seem strange, but I'm willing to bet that a woman in your family has done this before. Maybe not your aunts or grandmother, but in past generations, womb steaming was women's original feminine care and medicine.

Plants, which predate modern-day pills, were how our ancestors helped their bodies heal. They paid careful attention to their particular issue or need, picked local herbs, prepared a fire, heated water, and found a safe way to expose themselves to the steam. Whether through Swedish saunas, Native American sweat lodges, Moroccan hammam bath houses, or Korean spas, steam has been a healing tool for those who came before you.

Not sure where to start? As long as you have permission to make tea and handle hot water, preparing a steam session is as easy as finding the right pot or bowl to use. For starters, for this special act, you can't just go grabbing kitchen bowls or pots without asking first. Your steaming pot or bowl will be just for steaming, so no sneaking off with a ceramic casserole dish or mixing bowl and trying to return it to the kitchen unnoticed. If there's a stainless steel pot, ceramic bowl, or clay pot that is no longer used for cooking, these options would be great. If you have an electric kettle, it's really easy to heat the water in whatever space you feel is most private or suitable for your steam session.

For steaming, use a source of water that is safe to drink. For many, that would be tap water, but if you're not allowed to brush your teeth with the tap water in your home, it's safer to use filtered or bottled water.

What you'll need:

- About a quart or liter of water
- 1 Tbsp of sea salt or apple cider vinegar (optional)
- 1 Tbsp (dried) or ½ cup (fresh) of an herb, such as mint (optional)

Method:
Once your water is boiled, you can choose to add 1 tablespoon of sea salt or apple cider vinegar and then wait until the steam feels warm enough to hold your hand over it comfortably.
If you want to add a pleasant-smelling herb, mint is always a good option. Add 1 tablespoon of dried mint or ½ cup of fresh mint to your water, then let your pot or bowl sit covered for about 10 minutes before checking if the steam is comfortably warm. All of those options are a good starting point and don't require in-depth knowledge of herbs and what they do.

Always place your hand above the steam first to ensure it's not too hot. Your vulva is way more sensitive than your hand, so steam should feel warm and soothing, never hot or scalding. To position yourself safely over the steam, you can ask your parents to buy or build a steaming stool or sauna box for you. Both options have an opening that you sit over so the steam can reach your vulva while you sit comfortably. A second option is to sit on a low footstool or a high cushion. Place a clean towel down for your seat, wear a large skirt, or wrap yourself with a blanket, and tuck the pot or bowl of steam between your feet. Alternatively, you can wrap a towel around your steaming pot or bowl, place it between your knees and rest your elbows or head on a cushion, bed, chair, or couch nearby.

A last resort option is the toilet. You have to clean it before placing your pot of tea inside the toilet bowl. Then, all you have to do is sit on the toilet. If you're in a crowded home, the bathroom might be the most accessible location to steam. Just make sure that you try to urinate before cleaning the toilet because when steam touches your urethra (the opening where urine comes out), you might feel the urge to pee. I recommend steaming for only 10 minutes unless a certified vaginal steaming or peristeam facilitator has advised otherwise. Learn more about how these practitioners can help you in Dive Deeper section's *"Not Just Hot Air, Interview with Peristeam Hydrotherapist Keli Garza"* on page 124.

When we steam for the one to three days leading up to our period and one to three days after our period ends, we support the gentle cleansing action of our monthly period. Adding warmth helps to clear out blood from a previous period that got stuck along the way. Also, the boost in warmth helps your period to flow without cramping, spotting, or becoming brown. Give it a try, and note in your journal how steaming affects your next period.

2. Womb Massage

If steaming doesn't sound like your cup of tea, no worries. You can add warmth and improve circulation to your uterus with your own two hands. Grab some olive, coconut, jojoba oil, or shea butter. Lay yourself down in a quiet and comfy space. If your oil was stored in the fridge, you can place a small amount in a teacup and then place your teacup in a bowl of hot (not boiled) water to warm the oil. We never boil oil directly or overheat it. Allow yourself to relax by breathing slowly through your nose, holding for four counts, and then out through your mouth. Let this breath calm and relax your mind.

When you're ready, add a small amount of oil to the palm of your hand and rub the warm oil between your palms. Rest your hands gently on your abdomen with one hand above and one hand below your belly button. Begin to move your hands in counter-clockwise circles beginning around your belly button. Massage yourself slowly with firm, loving strokes moving outward to large circles reaching your ribs to your hips. Repeat this slowly for up to ten minutes. As you massage, think of a beautiful wish, prayer, or affirmation you want to offer your womb.

Examples of affirmations include:

My womb is full of light and love

I release pain, shame, and fear from my blessed womb

My womb is the birthplace of my dreams, goals, and future family

My womb is my friend, not my enemy

Having a womb is a blessing

I can have peaceful periods every single month

My period is teaching me how to better care for myself

When you're finished, close your eyes and pay attention to the sensations you feel in your body. Do you feel lighter? Warmer? Sleepy? Energized? Take note and add it to your period journal. This massage technique can be done any time of the month, before, during, or after your period. Consider it to be a tool in your period care toolbox.

3. Castor Oil Packs

If you find that your period tends to have a lot of clumps or clots, you can try using a castor oil pack. Castor oil has been used for generations to increase blood flow to the body. Applying the oil to our lower abdomen can help break up large clots or clumps of tissue that our uterus works hard to expel when we're on our period. The easiest way to apply a castor oil pack is before bed. You can generously rub it all over your abdomen, cover the area with a wool or flannel cloth, then wrap a towel around the pack from belly to back and sleep with it on. Another option is to place a heating pad over the wool or flannel cloth after you've applied castor oil to your abdomen.

If you've never used castor oil before, try adding a few drops to your skin and observing if you react within 24 hours. If you're allergic to castor oil, a small amount should show a reaction, so be sure to check before applying more.

4. Hip Tying

Even without castor oil, wrapping the lower abdomen is a traditional practice still used today to keep the womb warm during menstruation. Whether you use a *lappa*, *faja*, or *bengkung*, the goal is not to squeeze your waist like shapewear. Wrapping keeps the hips and lower back supported from your pelvis upward. Some wraps extend from the hip bones to the ribcage, while others are only applied between the pubic area and the belly button. Wearing your waist wrap while upright and active can be a powerful reminder for yourself and others that your womb requires special care, especially during your period. There is no need to wear a waist wrap while resting and relaxing.

5. Dancing

Another way to relieve stress and tension in your pelvis, increase warmth and circulation, and relieve pain is simply dancing. Whether you choose to move to music or the drum of your own beating heart, movements like bouncing, rocking, shaking, and swaying literally help relieve stress. And if we target those movements in our hips, we get to massage our womb internally by letting our pelvic muscles expand and contract around it. This doesn't require professional dance skills or training. Just move and have fun doing it!

Ok. Maybe what I've shared above sounds new and kinda weird to you. But that's alright. I want to imagine that you came over to my house, and I laid out a beautiful buffet spread for you. The dishes might be new to you, but see if any of the dishes intrigues you or makes you feel curious to try. This is how I want you to approach these practices and ideas. If it doesn't sound appealing, it might not be for you at this time. You can always come back and try it later.

However, if you know that you're really committed to never going back to painful, heavy, or difficult periods and PMS, it will take a few conscious steps and self-care practices every day of the month. But once they become a part of your lifestyle, peaceful period living will become your norm and way of life. The next chapter will show you how.

CHAPTER RECAP:

Period symptoms are our body's way of getting our attention and telling us that our needs aren't being met.

The 5 Peaceful Period Practices are:
1. Nourishing Food
2. Warmth
3. Rest
4. Relaxation
5. Unplug

Womb Wellness Practices that have helped women have peaceful periods for generations include:
1. Womb Steaming
2. Womb Massage
3. Castor Oil Packs
4. Hip Tying
5. Dancing

Journal Prompt:

If your womb was a room, describe what it would look and feel like. What color(s) would you use to draw your womb? What objects would you use to decorate your 'womb room'? Sketch your womb room, if you like.

CHAPTER 5:
WHY DO I FEEL SO DIFFERENT EVERY WEEK?

When we look at nature, we notice special seasons to mark the appearance of nesting birds, creeping insects, and our favorite fruits. Leaves change color as the weather shifts from warm to cold, and trees become bare in the winter. It would be strange for trees and plants to remain the same every day of every month, despite the weather changing. Part of their 'aliveness' is their ability to change with the environment. Like nature, the body also shifts to different seasons throughout every menstrual cycle.

Maybe you've only recognized two seasons in your body— period and no period. But have you ever noticed feeling a little irritable the week before your period or a burst of energy a week or two after your period has ended? If you were to write down or track when your period comes every month, you might notice some very interesting patterns over the course of the month.

Daily Clock

Let's first understand the daily rhythm that all human beings share— the circadian rhythm. Like an internal clock, your circadian rhythm nudges you to wake up as the sun rises and lulls you to slow down after the sun sets. Many of us can't feel those daily nudges because our days have become longer than before. Electricity allows us to artificially have "daylight" all night long, both indoors and outdoors. Have you ever been to my hometown of New York City? It's called "the city that never sleeps" and a perfect example of this is in central Manhattan. Times Square is an area lit with glaring bright lights throughout the entire night. It's always as lit as if it's the middle of a sunny day. Can you imagine how confused your body would be about when to rest if the lights never went out?

Another major reason many of our daily rhythms are thrown off is the use of screens like televisions, computers, tablets, and phones just before bed. The light emitted from our devices can trick our brains into mistaking it for sunlight, which can make it hard to wind down after a movie or video chat. It makes no sense to your brain to go from bright lights to lights out at the tap of a button. Especially if you're watching something interesting or texting a close friend after dark, you might be too excited to wind down at a reasonable hour.

Monthly Clock

Once you start menstruating or having a period, you now have another internal clock that your body responds to. It's called an infradian rhythm, and it cycles about once per lunar month or moon cycle. I specify the lunar month because the moon takes 29 or 30 days to complete its cycle. It is born as a crescent moon, grows or waxes until it reaches full illumination, and then wanes until it seems to disappear. Similarly, a healthy period tends to arrive every 28 to 30 days, which is controlled by your infradian rhythm. Your body is designed to pass through distinct phases just like the moon and weather seasons.

Moon Cycles

The words "month," "menstruation," "menarche," and "menopause" are linguistically connected to the moon, but that's not the only connection. Some cultures historically saw menstruation as a time of spiritual significance where wisdom and truth are revealed in dreams, intuition, and reflection. For this reason, many women would gather in special tents or lodges while menstruating to be protected and cared for during this sacred time. Communities would gather around them to hear what messages they had to share with the collective.

Additionally, some cultures place specific emphasis on the timing of one's period beginning with either the new moon or full moon. This occurrence has become less common due to artificial light exposure at night, but you might find it interesting to see what moon phase your own period correlates to every month.

Seasonal Shifts

The seasons of the year have unique characteristics, moods, and strengths. You don't wear the same clothes in the summer that you wear in the winter, and neither should you eat the same foods in the spring that you would in the fall. When we observe nature, we know there is a peak time for a particular food because the weather provides what that specific food needs to ripen. Your hormones are like the weather forecast— they set the environment for some of your unique gifts or 'fruits' to ripen too. When our hormones are out of balance, it can be challenging to know when and what you should be growing or expecting to harvest.

Winter

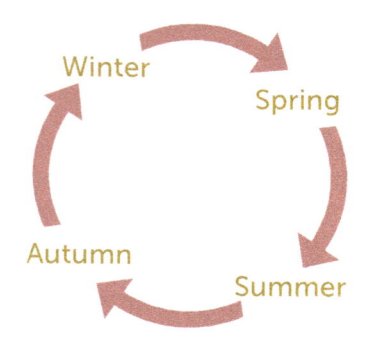

Spring

Summer

Autumn

To clarify what I mean, let's introduce our hormonal phases as seasons. We'll start with the winter, which correlates with your menstrual phase because the first day of your period is considered day 1 of your menstrual cycle.

Menstrual Phase: Your Inner Winter

During your period, have you ever felt unable to pay attention to the outer world? Have you ever just wanted to rest and observe your inner world? Well, winter is a season of turning inward and releasing. In regions of the world where we observe cold weather in the winter, we warm our bodies with blankets, warm beverages, stews, and soups. Trees almost look lifeless as all leaves shed, and their energy turns within. It benefits your body to rest in this phase- when you're on your period. Your body has built up extra blood volume and tissue in preparation for this shedding. Pushing yourself too hard while bleeding can make you feel exhausted.

If you haven't nourished yourself with iron-rich foods like greens, dried fruits, red meat, and beans or hydrated yourself with water, tea, and fruits, you might feel fatigued or in need of sweets to replenish your energy. Instead of reaching for sugar, pause and nourish yourself with fluid, food, and rest. If you find yourself craving chocolate, perhaps your body lost too much magnesium while preparing to menstruate. As I mentioned earlier, chocolate is derived from the cacao plant, which is rich in magnesium, so feel free to enjoy some dark chocolate to boost your magnesium. A few pieces of a dark chocolate bar with at least 60% cocoa can help meet your craving. Warm yourself to the soul by sipping on ginger tea or calm menstrual cramps with chamomile tea.

If you have an important decision to make, your period is the perfect time to take full advantage of your intuition or inner sense of knowing, helping you decide exactly what you do and don't want. Lower levels of estrogen and progesterone at this time help you to be neither too risky nor too cautious in your decision-making. So, tap into your inner wisdom and be guided to the best path forward.

> Did you know? When you're on your period, your spatial awareness skills are top-notch! This means you'll have a better sense of where you are in relation to objects around you than you would during another time of the month. This could be a great time to schedule a driving test, take a leisurely walk in new terrain, or work on an intricate puzzle.

Pre-Ovulatory Phase: Spring Has Sprung

Spring is your time to emerge. Your period is over, and if you rested well during your period, your energy should be on the rise. Ideally, you're ready to step out of hibernation and emerge into the wide world. An increase in estrogen makes you feel courageous and more confident. This is a great time to try new things, take risks, and dream BIG. How big? As big as your mind and heart can imagine. Hold a vision for what you'd like to accomplish this month, and don't be afraid to be bold. If you already made a vision board for the year, take a peak to be reminded of what you want to invite in your life and think about what you can do this month to get closer to attaining it. Nourishing herbal teas, like nettle and mint, can help you recover vitamins and minerals lost during your period.

After your 'winter' rest, your body is ready to move, so feel free to pick up your pace in movement. Your metabolism is lower at this point, so movement will help you maintain your spring energy throughout the day. New fitness practices will feel fun and refreshing. Your short-term memory boost in this phase will help you tackle new tasks and coordination.

Ovulatory Phase: Summertime

Life is in full bloom in the summer. Heat rises. Fruits ripen. Energy peaks. Similarly, your body is in its ripest season. One or two of your immature eggs has grown into full maturity and is ready to be ejected from one of your ovaries (remember the parachute?). Estrogen is at its highest concentration in your body, which makes you feel capable of great things and very social. A peak in testosterone helps you want to connect with others and feel energetic, as well as get closer to people who you really like.

Considering your biology in this season, it's important to think wisely about the company you keep. Your body might feel more drawn to socialize than at other times of the month, but that doesn't mean you should hang out with any and everyone. Make sure you're connecting with people who respect, uplift, and inspire you to be your best. Some notice that their ovulatory phase, or summer season, isn't ideal for making important life decisions because of how high estrogen levels are at this time. Remember, estrogen can make us feel comfortable with taking bigger risks, while progesterone can make us a bit more cautious and critical.

If you like intense exercise, the ovulatory phase is your season. Running, jumping, and pushing your physical limits are best done at this time. Similarly, if you like drinking fresh-pressed juices or eating large salad meals, this inner summer is the best time for it. Raw foods and the high fiber they contain will help your body get rid of all the estrogen you've used and move it out of your body to prevent hormonal imbalances from creeping up on you in the week before your period.

> **Did you know?** The verbal and social command centers of your brain are most active when you ovulate, so this is a great time to speak your mind, present your ideas, and connect with others.

Luteal Phase: Autumn

There's a shift when summer comes to an end. The temperature cools down, leaves start to change, and you know that winter will arrive soon. Seasonally, this is the time to collect your harvest, store food, and make sure everything you need to make it through the winter is readily available. Similarly, your energy should be turning inward, and your brain will find completing tasks, organizing, and spending time tending to your priorities very satisfying.

If you haven't been kind to your hormones all month, this is the time that imbalances will show up. Breast tenderness, bloating, and moodiness are generally the result of estrogen being much higher than progesterone during this season. Your body's metabolism and temperature rise, meaning you're using energy much quicker. In response, your body needs more calories (i.e., more food), so pay close attention to your meals and eat foods that will help sustain your energy, like whole grains, beans, and root vegetables.

Simple carbs like sugary treats and drinks, white bread, or white pasta aren't as helpful for blood sugar balance at this time, especially if they are not paired with a source of protein, like cheese, legumes, meats, nuts, seeds, or beans. Your blood sugar is naturally lower, and cortisol, one of your stress management hormones, is naturally higher in the luteal phase. If you don't feed your body adequately, the all-too-frightening "hangry monster" might emerge.

When your hormones are in balance, you should feel the effect of progesterone. This 'chilled-out' hormone is highest in your luteal phase. Progesterone helps you think cautiously and practically about what needs to be done and how to organize yourself to complete your tasks. Setting boundaries and making time to wrap up projects that interest you are important in this season. Progesterone helps us move towards closure, problem-solving, and completion.

It takes one whole year to experience the Earth's four seasons. However, we have the opportunity to experience the energy of all these seasons every month. If remembering where you're at in your menstrual cycle and season seems too overwhelming, I'll give you a more simplified way of approaching this. You can also find a Seasonal Self-Care Reference Chart in the Resource Hub on page 132.

As an alternative to the four-season perspective of looking at your cycle, we can split your menstrual cycle into two halves: period to ovulation and after ovulation to period.

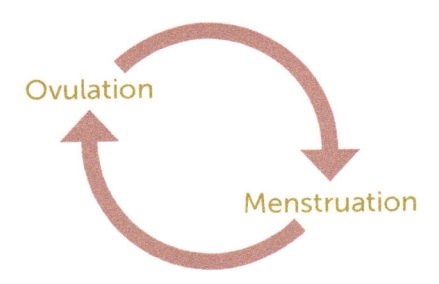

Ovulation

Menstruation

Once your period ends, your energy will increase up until ovulation. This is a great time to fill up on fruits and vegetables, both lightly cooked and raw. Physical strength, socialization, and communication are your prime superpowers at this time.

After you've ovulated, your energy should slowly turn inward, and your mind may become more focused on completing tasks and deeply reflecting on them. Warmer foods that are roasted, stewed, and slow-cooked will be helpful, particularly root vegetables, like sweet potatoes and beets, and whole grains, like brown rice and buckwheat.

When you're looking for a clue that ovulation is approaching, check your undies. You should notice clear and stretchy cervical mucus similar to uncooked egg whites. You may notice this fertile fluid when you wipe your vulva after using the bathroom or feel watery wetness in your underwear.

A more accurate way to know exactly if and when you've ovulated is by checking your basal body temperature every morning before you get out of bed. Once your body has been asleep for at least five hours, your body temperature reaches its lowest point, which tells us a lot about your metabolism or how quickly you're taking energy from your food. If we make a chart with our morning temperatures, we would see a noticeable jump in our daily temperature after ovulation. That temperature shift should remain slightly higher for a few days, telling us that an egg has been released and we are now making progesterone, a heat-releasing hormone. Your body temperature is raised until progesterone production drops at the start of your period. We'll learn more about period tracking in Chapter 11.

CHAPTER RECAP:

- The body is not designed to feel, look, or be the same every single day.
- By understanding our menstrual seasons, we can plan our schedule around our body's strengths and needs.
- It is normal to expect changes in appetite, appearance, energy, focus, and fitness throughout the month.
- See the Seasonal Self-Care Reference Chart in the Resource Hub on page 132.

Journal Prompt:
What color, symbol, or image would you use to represent each menstrual season? Add them in the following chart.

Winter   Spring

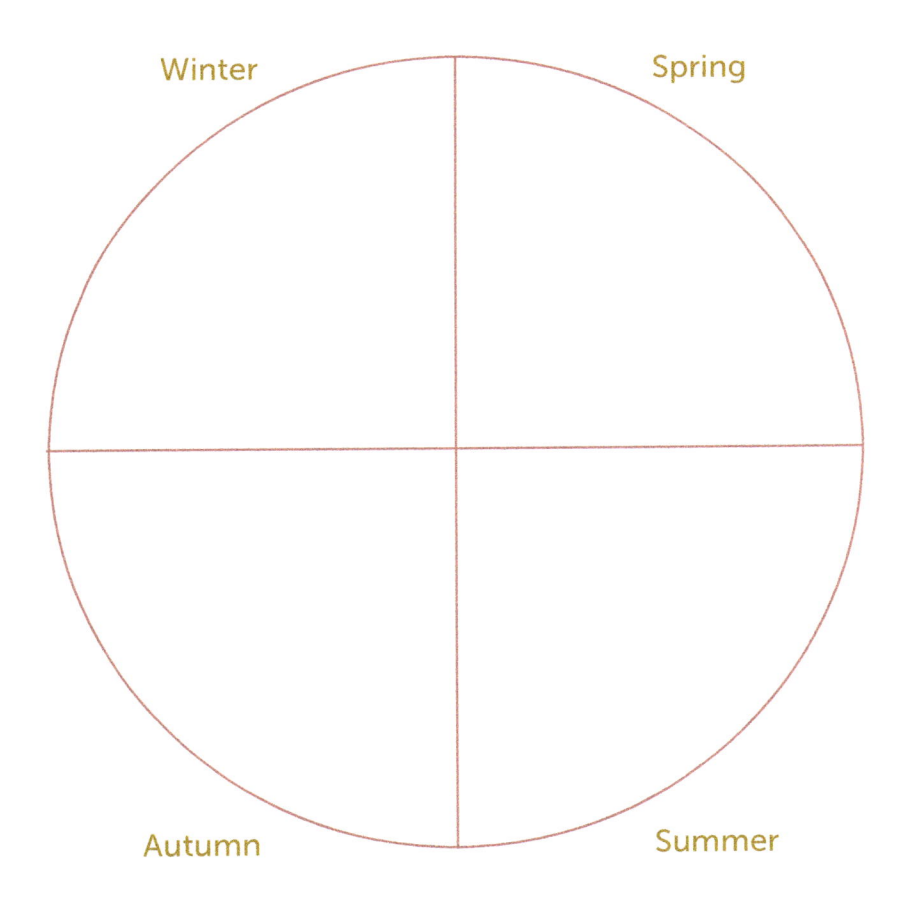

Autumn   Summer

CHAPTER 6:
PINK, BROWN, STICKY, WATERY: WHY IS MY PERIOD LIKE THIS?

Your period is not only power— it's vital information about your health. Everything from when it starts to how it flows is data worth tracking. When we take note of what's going on with our periods, we can identify when our choices positively or negatively affect our periods. This allows us to make choices and changes with full awareness of the consequences they bring, both good and not-so-good. And you know what's so beautiful about your period? If things didn't go so well in one month, you have another month to try again.

In the practice of Peristeam Hydrotherapy, which uses Traditional Chinese Medicine assessment principles, periods are evaluated through the lens of seven key period imbalances. These imbalances are not diagnoses but can help you evaluate your monthly period like a report card. When in balance, we can describe a balanced and healthy menstrual cycle as:

- A four-day menstrual flow
- Being cranberry red in color from start to finish
- Having a steady flow like maple syrup— neither watery, sticky, clotted, or thick
- Without cramping, disruptive pain or discomfort, or PMS (premenstrual syndrome) symptoms
- Occurring every 28-30 days
- With noticeable clear, stretchy, and slippery cervical mucus at the time of ovulation (around mid-way between periods)

Does that sound like a unicorn period to you? Period discomfort and pain are so common that a pain-free period may sound like a stroke of luck. However, I have personally witnessed teens and women reduce their period pain and discomfort with the right support. Let's consider the above period like a true north on our compass. Now, I'll share the seven key period imbalances and what they might be trying to tell you.

1. Uterine Fatigue

Description:
When the uterus struggles to keep uterine arteries closed between periods.

Indicators:
- Menstrual cycles that are 27 days long or less
- Fresh red or pink spotting before or between periods
- Two periods in one month
- Spontaneous bleeding
- Irregular bleeding
- Flood bleeding that is heavy and difficult to stop
- Ongoing bleeding

Uterine Fatigue can be connected to overall fatigue or inadequate rest, as well as physical and emotional exhaustion. In this case, prioritizing rest and committing to self-care practices are important to protect your energy—both physical and emotional. Remember, the womb is considered to be like a second heart, so emotional upset can show up as premature bleeding, spotting, or heavy bleeding.

On a nutritional level, easy-to-digest foods, like slow-cooked stews and soups, can help to replenish your body's strength. Iron-rich foods like leafy greens, red meat, beans, and beets can help rebuild blood supply. Uterus-strengthening herbs like red raspberry leaf, astragalus, ginseng, and ashwagandha can be helpful teas to drink, as well as herbs that discourage heavy bleeding like yarrow, guava leaf, shepherd's purse, and mugwort. Always check with your parent, guardian, or medical provider for documented allergies before trying new herbal teas.

2. Uterine Stagnation

Description:
When the uterus has a build-up of old residue due to poor circulation or poor period care. This can occur when the liver is not functioning well, the body is cold, or there is something blocking or restricting blood flow.

Indicators:
- Menstrual cycles that are 31 days long or more

- Brown spotting before or after period
- Cramps or shooting pains
- Clots
- Dark menstrual flow that is brown, black, purple, or stringy
- Absent periods

Brown blood tells us that our blood circulation is a bit sluggish. It's been flowing too slowly or sitting for too long, so it may be a bit thicker and darker than ideal. This color has a message for you too. It means that your womb, and likely your whole body, needs more warmth, movement, and circulation. This might look like taking the steps instead of an elevator, keeping socks on your feet at night, or keeping your tummy covered when the weather outside is cool. Brown blood is definitely a flag saying, "Let's move it!".

Black blood is an SOS message calling for help. If your blood isn't fresh and flowing, we need to clear out the old blood and get your fresh blood flow moving again. Womb steaming before and after your period can be helpful here, as well as avoiding frozen and cold foods for a while.

A clotted flow also tells us that blood circulation is not ideal. Sometimes our blood makes clots to slow down very heavy bleeding. But those clots can also tell us that blood flow is so slow that it is clotting. Either way, clots are trying to get our attention, and our uterus might work especially hard to force them out by cramping or contracting. All the practices we discussed earlier that keep our wombs warm and blood flowing (see Chapter 4) will help relieve clotting.

3. Blood Deficiency
Description:
When the blood supply is low in nutrients, or the liver is unable to generate enough blood.

Indicators:
- Pale menstrual blood color
- Fatigue during or after period
- Light period flow

- Headaches
- Absent periods

Pale or pink blood tells us that something is missing and that there is a lack of healthy blood supply, likely because of inadequate nourishment from our food. It can even be an early sign of anemia, low iron in your blood. When we see pink blood, we need to think about how often and what we've been eating. If you struggle with your body image or eating enough food, a pink period tells us that your body needs more support, like rest and nutrition. Otherwise, your period may go missing. And if you think a disappearing act would be great news for you, remember this— no period means no ovulation.

No ovulation means you don't have all the superpowers progesterone offers. Remember your chill chick? Progesterone won't show up and give you all of the mood-calming, self-protective, and organizational superpowers that help you feel like your feet are firmly planted on the ground. If you struggle with anxiety or feeling overwhelmed, you can't afford to miss out on your monthly dose of progesterone.

A watery menstrual flow or a period that only shows up as spotting without establishing a flow steady enough to require a period product might be telling us that we need more nutrition and nourishment. By increasing the quantity and quality of foods we eat, we can build more blood for a healthy flow. However, if our digestion is weak, and we're not extracting all the nutrients from our food, this can also be a cause of blood deficiency.

4. Dampness
Description:
An excess of mucus in the uterus that drains as discharge or accumulates inside.

Indicators:
- Irregular discharge that is white, yellow, green, or blood-tinted
- Sticky menstrual flow

A sticky flow can mean that we have a lot of mucus in our bodies. If you tend to eat a lot of sugar, dairy, or gluten, these may be the culprits. So try cutting back on those and notice if the stickiness resolves. Special attention should be given to personal hygiene in this case, as some vaginal discharge can irritate the skin. Until irritating discharge clears, you might want to wear non-toxic panty liners or change your underwear more frequently to avoid discomfort.

Alongside dietary changes, womb steaming can be a helpful ally in clearing out irregular discharge, much like how the steam of a hot shower can help drain a congested nose. If you notice a foul-smelling odor, itching, a burning sensation, or rash, you might have a vaginal infection that needs special attention. See Chapter 7 for some early interventions of support.

5. Dryness
Description:
A dehydrated and dry internal climate.

Indicators:
- Vaginal dryness
- Night sweats
- Thirst
- Constipation
- Dryness
- Flaky or chalky vaginal discharge
- Headaches

Dry or flaky discharge and menstrual flow tell us that we need more hydration. Aside from guzzling water, we can support hydration in the body with raw fruits and vegetables and slippery, gelatinous foods. Ideal hydrating foods are anything stretchy and slippery, like porridge, pudding, okra, or tapioca (boba tea is a personal favorite).

Our kidneys are key players in keeping our body hydrated, and we can support kidney function with herbs like hibiscus, watercress, oat straw, and shatavari.

6. Excess Heat
Description:
An excess of warmth in the internal climate.

Indicators:
- Hot flashes
- Night sweats
- Infections
- Fevers
- Rashes

While some think hot flashes and night sweats are just for menopausal folks, the reality is that even teens can find themselves feeling suddenly overheated or waking up in a pool of sweat. This can be more noticeable in the luteal phase, before your period, when progesterone raises our basal body temperature and can make us feel a bit warmer than usual.

Moisturizing herbs like calendula, comfrey, milk thistle, and mint can help cool the body. Even if you prepare these herbs as a hot tea, the herb by its nature will still have a cooling effect on the body. Alternatively, these herbs can be made as iced tea in warmer months. The cooling foods mentioned above for dryness will also be helpful here.

Interestingly, sometimes unexpressed anger and rage can raise our overall sense of warmth in the body, so practices like relaxation and deep breathing can have a cooling effect too.

7. Weak Digestion
Description:
Challenges related to digestion, elimination, and/or nutrient extraction.

Indicators:
- Nausea
- Vomiting
- Abdominal Bloating
- Diarrhea
- Constipation
- Gas

Our ability to digest food is often referred to as our digestive 'fire' or strength. When we cannot process and absorb nutrients we eat, our body may respond with the previously mentioned indicators. As a result, we might not be able to nourish our blood supply or overall health adequately. Acupuncturists can be helpful allies in pinpointing the root cause of weak digestion and identifying which of your organs most need support.

Mindful eating practices can be a helpful start on the road to better digestion. Many say digestion begins in the mouth, but even before that, the sight and smell of what we are about to eat prepares our body for the meal ahead. Taking time to really savor and experience your meal without distraction and chewing each bite of food 15-30 times might ease gas and bloating. However, some might benefit from more focused support. This is where an acupuncturist or functional nutritionist can be wonderfully helpful.

Mind Your Flow

When you track your period, it's important to take notes about your symptoms, menstrual flow color, and consistency. It is also helpful to track how often you change your period products. A healthy amount of flow would require you to change your pad, period panties, or tampons about once every four hours. Changing more frequently indicates a heavy flow, while less often indicates a light flow. A medium flow (changing your period products about once every four hours) is ideal for the first two to three days of your period. By day 3 or 4, the flow should begin to decrease before stopping completely.

Four is also a helpful number to remember regarding how many days you bleed. A four-day flow without spotting is best. Spotting is common, but multiple days of spotting aren't ideal (and frankly annoying). If your period begins with a day or two of dark red or brown spotting, it could be slow-moving or leftover blood from your previous cycle. However, three or more days of spotting before or after your period might mean that your progesterone levels are dropping too soon, or there may be an underlying condition that needs to be investigated. Spotting during times of high stress can happen, but if you're tracking more than three days of spotting regularly, consider talking to an acupuncturist, functional medicine practitioner, naturopathic practitioner, Ayurvedic practitioner, or a Peristeam Hydrotherapist.

Remember, what you observe in your body is all information. No judgment, just information. And this information tells you something about your body. What you do with that information is up to you.

CHAPTER RECAP:

- The colors and consistencies of our periods tell us important information about our health.
- Tracking how often you change your period products is a helpful way to monitor how much you're bleeding every month.
- A healthy period generally begins and ends with fresh, red, flowing blood and lasts about four days.

Journal Prompt:
Create a color chart with colored pencils, crayons, or paints ranging from pale pink to black. Label each period color to remember what it might mean.

Red	
Pink	
Brown	
Black	

CHAPTER 7:
SLIPPERY, STICKY, CREAMY: WHAT'S GOING ON IN MY UNDERWEAR?

What is commonly referred to as vaginal discharge can be better understood as cervical liquid or mucus. A discharge can sometimes refer to the release of an unpleasant or unwanted liquid, perhaps due to an infection or injury. But cervical mucus is a natural gel made of mostly water, mucus, enzymes, and minerals that change in response to your hormone levels, different types of medication, and other factors. Estrogen increases this mucus production in your cervix. It plays a critical role in helping fertilization and is perfectly normal.

For starters, your cervix is the base of your womb or uterus. Shaped like a small donut, it opens to release menstrual blood. Throughout the menstrual cycle, mucus at the cervix changes in response to the levels of hormones in your body. You'll often notice cervical mucus when wiping yourself in the bathroom or on your underwear throughout the day. After your period ends, you may not notice much, but as estrogen levels rise, you might eventually start to see creamy cervical mucus with the texture of lotion.

When estrogen peaks around ovulation, cervical mucus is usually more noticeable, slippery, and abundant. The type of mucus we expect to see around ovulation is very clear and stretchy, with no color or odor. If you were to stretch it between your fingers (make sure they're clean), the mucus could stretch more than an inch without snapping. Even though cervical mucus is made up of about 90% water, the type of mucus we see around the time of ovulation is up to 99% water, so its presence is quite noticeable and significant. It may leave a round-edged wet spot in your underwear because it's so watery. After an egg is released, this mucus can change to a more sticky consistency before it eventually dries out.

Clear, watery, and slippery fertile cervical mucus creates an ideal environment for fertilization to occur. Fertilization means that sperm, the male seed of life, has successfully reached a released egg within the female body. The vagina generally has an acidic pH, which sperm cannot survive in. But fertile cervical mucus is alkaline, which is the opposite of acidic, so it can keep sperm alive for up to five days by protecting it and preparing it to reach the egg released during ovulation. Sticky, unfertile cervical mucus acts like a net that prevents sperm from getting too far, which is why it wouldn't make sense to see unfertile mucus during ovulation time. Progesterone produced after ovulation can make our cervical mucus stickier and dry out as we pass ovulation and get closer to our period.

WHAT GOES IN

Other factors can impact the pattern of cervical mucus you see. If you eat mucus-forming foods, like some forms of dairy, soy, sugar, and gluten, you might regularly see sticky or creamy mucus, which makes identifying a pattern very challenging.

After our period, we expect to see little to no cervical mucus before it approaches a slippery consistency around ovulation, and then becomes dry again. If you're under stress or not having regular bowel movements, your estrogen levels might be elevated, which can cause a lot of cervical mucus. If you never see cervical mucus, perhaps your body isn't making enough estrogen to produce fertile-quality cervical mucus.

The point here is not to be afraid when you find moisture in your underwear. As long as the odor doesn't smell strange or offensive, there is no cause for alarm. However, if there is a foul odor that smells fishy, yeasty like bread, or off-putting like ammonia, there may be some unwelcome bacteria, yeasts, or viruses making a home in your vagina.

If you suspect you have an infection, don't panic! Stress only makes our body less capable of repairing itself. Most of us will experience some form of infection in our lives and most of these are treatable. If something doesn't feel quite right, pause, take a deep breath and get clear on what's happening.

- What sensations do you feel?
- What scents do you smell?
- How would you describe your experience?
- When did you first notice some discomfort?

Find a quiet place and a handheld mirror for a vulva check. Even if you don't suspect that something is wrong, routine vulva checks help you establish a baseline for what your normal healthy vulva looks like.

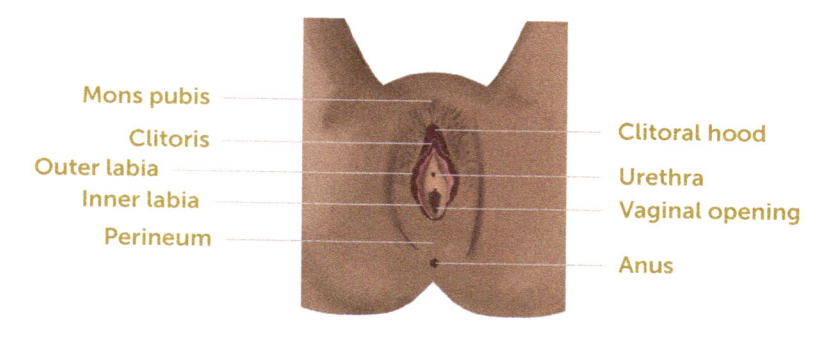

Mons pubis
Clitoris
Outer labia
Inner labia
Perineum

Clitoral hood
Urethra
Vaginal opening
Anus

What to look for during your vulva check:

- Check the color of your labia or vulva lips. What color do you notice? Blood-rich tissue of the inner labia should be pink in color.
- Look for bumps, cuts, sores, ingrown hairs, or changes in texture.
- Check the appearance and scent of your cervical mucus or discharge. Wipe with a clean tissue paper or clean finger and examine. Is the scent pleasant to you? Offensive? What would you compare the scent to? What does your cervical mucus or discharge look like?

The types of vaginal discharge that we want to pay close attention to and discuss with a parent or guardian are:

- foul-smelling
- clumpy
- colored (yellow, gray, or green)

Much like a cold, you can begin to treat an infection at home before running straight to a doctor. If you feel discomfort inside your vagina or on your vulva, avoid covering up unpleasant odors with scented feminine hygiene products, like douches, feminine sprays, or fragranced panty liners. Scented products can be irritating and introduce unnecessary chemicals to an already delicate environment. This is why a new laundry detergent or body soap can sometimes cause vaginal irritation. Look for hypo-allergenic, unscented soaps for your body and laundry, especially if you feel discomfort.

Cleanse your vulva (especially where pubic hair normally grows) with mild, natural, unscented soap, then rinse and thoroughly pat dry with a clean towel before putting on clean, breathable cotton underwear during the day and sleeping without underwear at night. If the skin of your vulva feels irritated, wash your hands thoroughly and gently apply coconut oil to the area. Coconut oil is naturally antibacterial and nourishing to the skin (as long as you don't have an allergy!). Alternatively, you can apply pure shea butter. Avoid mucus-forming foods for a while, like sugar, white flour products, and those mentioned above. And remember to never touch your private parts without properly washing your hands first.

If an unpleasant odor persists, consider a warm, herbal bath prepared with a handful of dried peppermint, rosemary, and/or lavender. Be sure to clean the tub thoroughly before preparing your bath, and avoid scented or colored bath products. If the discomfort feels more internal than external, you can try vaginal steaming using the same herbs (peppermint, rosemary, and/or lavender). Go to Chapter 4 for full steaming instructions. Please note that womb or vaginal steaming should never be done while menstruating or experiencing a burning itch.

Both an herbal bath and vaginal steam can help clear out irregular discharge after a few consecutive days of use, but also speak with a medical care provider you trust if your discomfort persists. Irregular discharge can be described as thick, foul-smelling, colored (gray, yellow, or green), or clumpy, like cottage cheese. Don't suffer through strange smells, itching, or irritation in silence.

Peaceful Panties

To prevent vaginal discomfort, wear comfortable underwear made of natural fibers like cotton, bamboo, or wool, and change your underwear daily. After an entire day of wearing underwear, give your vulva a breather by sleeping without them. Practice good hygiene by showering with natural soaps and keeping perfumed body products away from your vagina. Artificial colors or scents can irritate your very sensitive body parts. Avoid douching (forcing water inside of your vagina), which can wash away the good natural bacteria that help your body resist bad bacteria.

Remember, a healthy vagina, like every other part of your body, benefits from abundant water, fresh fruits and vegetables, wholesome foods, and herbal teas. A diet based on processed foods, fast food, and junk food will most likely interfere with your ability to have a healthy body, mind, or period, so choose your foods wisely.

CHAPTER RECAP:

- Paying attention to the consistency of your cervical mucus can help you understand what foods to eat or avoid.
- There are ways to treat vaginal discomfort and infections at home, though seeing a professional might be necessary if the problem persists.
- Feminine hygiene is not douches, sprays, and scented creams. Daily habits of cleanliness and self-care support a healthy vulva and vagina.

Journal Prompt:

What different types of cervical mucus have you noticed?

What vaginal discomforts have you or someone you've known experienced?

CHAPTER 8:
READY TO MEET YOUR PEACEFUL PERIOD BFFS?

The early years after your first period is like a test drive. Your ovaries are learning how to communicate with your brain and vice versa. Together, they have to organize the intricate sequence of events that allow your body to ovulate, menstruate, and everything in between. While figuring out how much of each hormone is required for all of these tasks, sometimes hitting the target amounts can make periods a bit awkward for teenagers. They may not come regularly or might be too heavy or too light. Combined with some typical teenage habits, like skipping meals, staying up late, and binging on junk food, your hormones might feel like you've been yanked onto a wild roller coaster ride. However, you have two peaceful period BFFs, and if you manage them well, your hormones can be well-balanced. Meet insulin and cortisol.

STAYING SAFE

Your ability to ovulate and menstruate means your body believes you are mature and healthy enough to reproduce. Your brain constantly scans for danger and signals to decide if you are safe. Two main ways our body perceives safety and security are stable blood sugar and well-managed stress. Stable blood sugar is managed by insulin and tells your body that you have access to enough food. Well-managed stress is impacted by cortisol and tells your body that you're not in danger, fighting or running to protect your life. When your body doesn't perceive stable blood sugar or well-managed stress, it may believe that your environment is not safe enough for a new egg to be released. Your body may think there are insufficient resources to support a new life or that it doesn't have a good chance of survival.

No egg means no period, right? Most of the time, yes. But no period means your body is not fully accessing all the superpowers of your menstrual cycle. Having no period may sound good, but I promise you that going long spans without menstruating means there is a problem. It might mean your body is not getting all the nutrients it needs, your weight is too high or low, you're experiencing too much stress, or some of your organs need more support. No ovulation means you're more likely to experience acne, difficulty losing weight, bloating, headaches, and mood swings. The longer your period goes missing in action, the more time and effort it will take to bring back a healthy, regular period. Even worse is that your risk of developing osteoporosis (loss of bone density), heart disease, diabetes, and cancer later in life increases when you don't ovulate regularly.

When your body feels regularly fed, rested, and well-cared for, you're more likely to see a consistent period pattern on a month-to-month basis. Being able to anticipate when your period is coming helps you plan ahead and not be surprised by the arrival of your period. And when it does arrive, a healthy period won't have you feeling like you're bleeding your life away or suffering in pain. So, let's figure out how to give your body the message that you're healthy enough to have a regular period and ovulate.

CHECK YOUR FUEL

To stabilize your blood sugar and be an ally to our BFF insulin, we need to start our day with a balanced breakfast. What does that look like? A bowl of cereal? A granola bar to go? Your favorite latte? Not quite. To jump-start your body after (hopefully) an entire night of rest, we need fuel that is going to set the foundation for the rest of our day. We start by hydrating ourselves with water — not juice or coffee — to jump-start our body's digestion. Drinking water when we wake up helps to cleanse our bodies and encourages a bowel movement before we get busy with our day.

Within the first 1-2 hours of your day, prioritize a breakfast centered around a protein source like eggs, beans, meat, or whole grains. Aim for animal products that are organic, free-range, and humanely raised because conventional meat and dairy in large supermarkets might be sourced from factory farms that inject their animals with antibiotics and growth hormones. Antibiotics prevent animals from getting sick, which is hard to avoid when they live indoors in cramped spaces. Growth hormones make animals grow quicker and bigger so they can produce more milk and be sold at a higher weight. Unfortunately, whatever an animal eats or takes as medicine impacts our health and can disrupt our natural hormonal balance. If you don't have access to high-quality, well-sourced animal products, I'd highly recommend experimenting with vegetarian or plant-based options.

Examples of quick breakfast meals are:
- Free-range scrambled eggs with avocado on sourdough bread
- Organic oatmeal with almond butter and hemp seeds
- Blueberry chickpea (flour) pancakes with maple syrup
- Baked beans, sausages, and veggies
- Lentil dhal and whole grain paratha
- Amaranth porridge with cinnamon-stewed apples and yogurt

You can tell that you've nailed a well-balanced breakfast when you're not craving something sweet afterward or feeling the urge to snack within three hours after a meal. If your body wants something sweet at the end of a meal, it might be looking for more energy or food fuel. Sweet foods give your body a quick and easy energy rush, but they are best paired with fat or protein to avoid your blood sugar rising too quickly and then crashing suddenly. The energy that sweets alone offer can't sustain you for long periods, which might make you feel jittery and irritable. White sugar, in particular, can reduce your immune system's ability to fight off harmful bacteria and viruses. Sweetener options that sustain your energy without temporarily reducing your immunity are dates, coconut sugar, honey, and maple syrup.

"But I'm Not Hungry."

Ok, Love. If food is the last thing on your mind in the morning, I hear you. After pressing the snooze button a few times on my alarm clock, my first thought every morning in high school was "Am I going to be late?". Year-round, I left home before sunrise to wait for the public bus and ride for 30 minutes before trekking about a mile uphill. Many mornings I would literally sprint to make sure I was in class before the first period bell rang at 7:08am.

My body intelligently suppressed my hunger, perceiving that I was too stressed or unsafe to pause and eat. Over time, this habit of hunger suppression can become our routine and because we probably wouldn't pause to eat anyway, our body can stop cueing when our blood sugar is low and we need to eat. Instead, our stress hormones keep us pushing until maybe mid-day when we are settled down enough to eat. I used to take great pride in my ability to go long stretches of time without feeling hungry and now see that I was running on stress hormones the entire time.

When you regularly fast or abstain from food for long periods of time, your organs scramble to figure out other sources of energy in the absence of food. Should we break down some fat or muscle for energy? Should we hold onto body fat because we're not sure how long this fast will last? Can we afford to ovulate this month? If you haven't eaten since the prior evening, the best gift you can give your blood sugar and hormones is breakfast. Even if you're not hungry, know that your body needs fuel and, with time, your body will start to stir your morning appetite again. Unregulated blood sugar makes hormonal issues much more complicated later in life. By addressing your lack of hunger now, your hormones will be better supported for years to come. And if cooking in the morning is really not an option, protein-rich bars or smoothies can fill the gap until you get around to eating.

> **Did you know?** Skipping breakfast is a common practice in Intermittent Fasting, a diet that involves limiting the timeframe in which you eat. Most studies on intermittent fasting have been conducted on males and show some health benefits. However, the stress of low blood sugar levels can be challenging to hormonal balance in our menstruating years.

Lunch should ideally be your largest meal of the day. If you love bread, pasta, or rice, try incorporating it into this mid-day meal, so you'll still have plenty of hours to digest it before bedtime. Healthy fats like avocados, nuts, olives, cheese, and oily fish can help you feel full until your next snack or mealtime.

If you need an afternoon snack, think of what will help you feel full until dinner. That might mean whole grain crackers and cheese, dates and pistachios, apples and nut butter, or bean-based chips.

Dinner should ideally not be your heaviest meal and not too close to bedtime. However, if you tend to eat late in the morning, a late meal or snack the night before might help your body have the fuel needed to start the day until you get around to eating. Simple meals like soups or stews with salad or roasted vegetables can be easily prepared. Whether your family generally gathers for lunch or dinner together, remember that eating with full presence, joy, and intention helps our bodies get all the delicious benefits from our meal. Regularly eating while on our phones or screens makes us more likely to eat mindlessly, not recognizing when we are full or enjoying our meal.

Food Drama

Most of the foods mentioned above would be considered anti-inflammatory, meaning that they don't create some kind of swelling and stress in the body. On the other hand, inflammatory foods can contribute to painful periods. The main culprits are processed (white) sugar, factory-farmed dairy, and caffeine. These three food types tend to disrupt your hormones and increase inflammation in your body.

Historically, humans ate sweet foods as they occurred seasonally and in nature. In our modern diet, we've learned how to separate sugar from its source and add it to foods that we eat daily. This overabundance of concentrated sugar can be a source of stress and inflammation in the body.

Similarly, dairy was traditionally consumed from locally raised animals, but now with mass production, dairy products must be pasteurized, or heated to a high temperature, such that helpful bacteria are destroyed. Getting rid of bacteria sounds great, but some good bacteria and enzymes help our bodies digest milk proteins. Without them, milk can be acidic to the body and create inflammation. Also, the type of cows and how they are raised can influence how our body responds to drinking milk. Some find A2 cow's milk, goat milk, or fermented dairy products easier to digest.

Caffeine naturally occurs in some plants and foods, but it's found most abundantly in coffee, black tea, energy drinks, and sodas. Caffeine has a diuretic effect on the body, meaning that it makes you urinate, or pee. It's also a stimulant that raises your cortisol level and creates a stress response in the body, similar to your fight or flight response in times of danger. Depending on caffeine to get you through the day will have you peeing away valuable vitamins and minerals while overworking your "in case of emergency" stress response system.

Additionally, foods like gluten (the part of flour made from grains that makes it so sticky), soy, and peanuts can also be inflammatory. So if you limit or remove one or more of these food items from your diet, observe how your period responds. Your period can be a powerful indicator of what is working well for your body and what is not.

Alternatives to sugar: honey, date syrup, maple syrup, monk fruit, stevia, and coconut sugar.

Alternatives to inflammatory dairy: raw dairy products, A2 milk, goat milk, coconut milk, and homemade nut milk.

Alternatives to grains with gluten: buckwheat, quinoa, oats, barley, brown rice, and rye.

Alternatives to wheat pasta: chickpea, buckwheat, or brown rice.

Alternatives to caffeine: roasted dandelion root, burdock root, kukicha, and maca root teas.

THE BALANCING ACT

Now, let's talk about the second BFF that keeps our hormones in balance: cortisol, our stress response hormone. Popular culture glorifies the young person who binges on energy drinks to stay up all night and caffeinates to stay up all day. The 'hustle' and 'grind' have been glamorized as the hallmarks of true dedication and work, but burnout and exhaustion are prevalent issues that are difficult to recuperate from. Instead, we can work smarter, not harder, when we balance work, play, recreation, and rest.

When we experience stress, our body creates cortisol which raises our blood pressure, increases our heart rate and breathing, and ensures adequate blood flows to our limbs in case we need to fight off a predator or flee from a dangerous enemy. Though we logically know the difference between a challenging exam and a life-threatening situation, the chemicals that surge through our body still interpret any perceived danger as critical danger and act accordingly. When your body is constantly pumped with stress hormones, you may find it hard to wake up in the morning or sleep at night. You may feel uneasy or anxious during the day and generally spend most of your time surviving rather than thriving.

When we're able to pause in moments of stress to breathe, calm ourselves, and reflect on the best course of action, we can prevent our bodies from freaking out. The ability to stop and think before reacting to a situation, even if it seems infuriating or humiliating, can be a powerful tool to keep our cool, avoid acting out in uncontrolled rage, or respond in a way that doesn't make the situation much worse.

However, there are some situations where healthy aggression is needed to protect you and keep you and others safe. This might look like making sure your facial expression and body language match what you're saying, raising your volume to be heard, or enforcing distance between yourself and a threatening person. When you feel uncertain about a situation or encounter, it's ok to be extra guarded and careful until you feel safe enough to let down your guard. It's important that we don't make assumptions about people based on learned biases and prejudice, but also know that your intuition, or sense of inner knowing, is valid too.

Setting boundaries for ourselves is another powerful stress management tool. Have you heard the phrase "No is a complete sentence?" This may not apply to your parents or in all situations, but when a peer asks you to do something that will create conflict for you, you can say no. When someone asks you to be available when you're usually asleep, you can say no. When you are asked to spend time with people that are not kind and compassionate towards you, you can say no. You can save yourself a lot of stress by saying no, instead of feeling coerced into a scenario that your gut instinct says isn't right.

If you feel your heart racing or stomach clenching when the thought of a certain person, place, or activity comes to mind, observe those feelings. Sift through which feelings might be trying to protect you from harm and which are connected to a new experience that feels strange. Think through the benefits and risks a situation offers, and choose the path that will result in the least regret and most contentment in your heart. People rarely regret doing the right thing. You can learn healthy ways to handle difficult emotions in the Resource Hub's *Emotional Release Technique by Dr. Nicole Monteiro* on page 134

As young people, we are often told what to do, and this might make it challenging to listen to our intuition or inner voice. Intuition is when our brain knows something without our conscious awareness, much like a reflex. It's a stroke of insight, a knowing, a feeling, alerting you even before you fully know and understand why. Breathing exercises and meditation can help quiet your mind and strengthen your ability to tune in with yourself. The more you're able to hear your heart, the less doubt you'll have in life when others want to tug you into their plan and agenda. By turning down the outer noise, you can better hear your voice and be guided by your inner light.

MOTIVATION TO MOVE
Exercise is another great way to manage stress, but don't go overboard or

muddle your intentions. The main reason to exercise should be to benefit your health and wellness. When you feel good inside your body, you can feel self-satisfaction and an overall good feeling, knowing you're helping your body feel its best. Some people exercise as a form of weight loss or body shaping, but remember *health and well-being* are much more attainable than trying to look like an imagined ideal. Loving yourself means accepting who you are, as you are, without conditions about who you should become. Whether curvy, medium, or slender in size; peachy, olive, caramel, or chocolate in complexion; find beauty in yourself first and foremost.

While we're on the topic, let's discuss beauty care products and how they impact your hormones.

Some chemicals in conventional hair and skin care products go beyond skin-deep. In our shampoos, conditioners, lotions, skin creams, deodorants, make-up, relaxers, perfumes, hair treatments, etc., there are chemicals that don't just linger on your scalp or skin surface but penetrate further into your body where they mimic estrogen and other hormones. By doing this, your body's own natural hormone production can be disrupted and get off-balance.

If you're wondering how this is possible, it's important to note that the beauty industry is not heavily regulated. There are more than 10,000 unique chemical ingredients in beauty products. That's a lot to keep track of, so they are not screened in the same way that foods and beverages are before being sold to the public.

CLEAN AND CUTE

So, what to do? If your current beauty care products have questionable ingredients (and they likely do), consider phasing them out by replacing them with non-toxic beauty care products. The Environmental Working Guide's Skin Deep ® Directory has an extensive list of products that can enhance your natural beauty without messing with your hormones, disrupting your period, or loading you with cancer-causing compounds.

Sometimes, wearable beauty products like waist trainers and body-slimming undergarments can impact our health too. Our abdomen is a bit like a balloon in that when you squeeze one part, pressure is forced to another part. When we constrict our waist and stomach to look slimmer, we push our uterus, bladder, and intestines downward, which can limit blood flow and weaken the ligaments and muscles that hold them in place.

As for footwear, regularly wearing high heels can tilt your pelvis forward, which can tip or shift your uterus too. Poor positioning of the uterus is one of the ways that blood supply can be compromised and stagnation can occur (see Chapter 6). If your heels are high enough to force your hips to rock up and down when you walk, try shortening them a bit or limiting how often or how long you wear high heels.

I don't share this to cramp your style or critique your fashion sense, but remember, there is no greater beauty than fully loving and inhabiting the unique human being that you are. If there is something that you find so despicable about your natural form that you want to permanently, not temporarily, change, sit with that idea for a bit. Ask yourself:

- How do I describe beauty? Where did I learn this description?
- Do I see myself as beautiful? Why or why not?
- Are there parts of my appearance that I want to enhance or totally erase?

THE BUSINESS OF BEAUTY

In an era of camera filters, airbrushed images, and AI art, we can get swept away in beauty standards that feel impossible to attain. And you know what, they are! Plastic surgery, tattooed eyebrows, lash extensions, and hired glam squads are just a few ways the $571.1 billion beauty industry profits off of each individual's insecurities. If you find yourself wanting to be other than who you are, take a break from the virtual world of celebrities and public figures. Instead, find yourself in the company of people who you genuinely see as beautiful and feel beautiful with.

If you struggle with your weight, first examine how you feel about your size. Are you comfortable with your level of physical activity? Are you experiencing health challenges or self-esteem issues concerning your weight? No matter your size, everyone can benefit from movement in whatever way suits their circumstances. If you haven't been as active as you like, walking daily is a great starting point that can be easy to maintain. Walking has been proven to not only help your health but also support a positive mood and mindset.

WORK OUT FOR WITHIN

If you want to try something more vigorous like running or team sports, these kinds of fitness activities can be empowering and help you discover your strength, tone your muscles, and work well with others. If you're the type who needs to be tricked into exercising, a dance class can be a fun way to keep your body moving and express your creativity without feeling like you're even working out. You could try an online class to start. However you choose to move your body, whether at home, in school, online, or at a gym, make sure you stay well-fed, hydrated, and rested to maximize your results.

Exercising on an empty stomach is like driving with an empty tank of fuel—you can't get too far. And when your period comes, remember to take a few days off from intense exercise to rest. When you're bleeding, it's best to rest deeply and move gently by choosing things like walking or stretching as your physical activity. If we continue with intensive exercise while on our period, we:

- run the risk of sweating away valuable vitamins and minerals that are needed to build back up our blood supply
- miss out on nature's opportunity for us to 'recharge' for the month
- are more likely to bleed longer and heavier because our womb's blood vessels are open while we bleed

After your period, you can return to more active forms of fitness. A healthy balance of rest and activity is important for maintaining health.

Physical activity, meditation, and deep breathing are all helpful tools for managing stress. When our bodies are stressed out, they don't function best, and they don't give priority to making sure our hormones are healthy. Remember what we said about ovulation? Your body can literally shut down the egg conveyor belt if it feels threatened or under attack.

LIGHTS OUT

A consistent bedtime, preferably by 10:00 PM, helps your body know when to rest and recharge. Sleeping in a (completely) dark room that is slightly cool in temperature and free of screens can help your mind do the deep work that it needs to do every night. Your brain is a powerhouse and we can best access its full capacity when we rest.

> Did you know? Female brains are about 10% smaller in size than male brains, yet function in more holistic and complex ways. Female brains need an average of 20 more minutes of sleep than the male brain to clear and process all of its data and prepare for a new day.

Give yourself one to two hours before bedtime to wind down through a nightly routine. Your routine can include a light snack, reading, a relaxing bath or shower, skin or hair care, journaling, or chatting with your loved ones. Think about what will help your mind ease into stillness and calm, and make them part of your nightly rhythm. Try to avoid screens before bedtime; the over-stimulation causes your brain to think it's not yet time to rest, being tricked into staying active longer.

Tips for limiting the effects of night-time screen use:

- Use blue light-blocking glasses or screen filters when viewing screens after dark. Blue light emitted from screens mimics sunlight, which can wake up your brain when it's time to rest.
- Turning on "Do not Disturb" or Airplane mode an hour before you plan to be asleep.
- Use an alarm clock instead of sleeping with your phone beside you.
- Expose your eyes to natural sunlight in the morning by gazing at the sky (not staring into the sun!) and letting sunrays caress your skin to help regulate your daily clock.
- Keep track of your screen use with a timer and be deliberate in setting limits for yourself, especially after dark.

CHAPTER RECAP:

- Stable blood sugar is one of the key ways we communicate safety to our bodies.
- Regular wholesome meals and adequate rest are how we let our bodies know that we are healthy enough to ovulate and have periods.
- Both moderate physical activity and regular night sleep help us manage stress and let our bodies know that we are safe.

Journal Prompt:

Describe a meal that keeps you full for 4-5 hours. When do you usually eat this meal? What's your favorite snack when you feel hungry between meals?

CHAPTER 9:
CRAVINGS AND CRASHES: WHAT AM I SUPPOSED TO EAT?

Your beautiful body needs quality fuel to do its job. Fast food and junk food are common teenage vices. Have you ever wondered why? After puberty, the pleasure receptors in your brain begin to increase, which means that you might find certain foods more enjoyable than before. Ripe fruits or your favorite home-cooked meal can give you all the good feels, but it's not likely that they'll compare to fried and processed foods that contain many flavor enhancers intended to get you hooked. Seasonings like MSG (mono-sodium glutamate) are added to foods to over-excite your brain's response to what you're eating. Processed foods intentionally have many preservatives and chemical additives that make them cheap to produce, addictively tasty, and stable on a supermarket shelf for months, if not years, after they're made. These newer ingredients are less recognizable to your body.

TAKE OUT THE TRASH
For centuries, humans have eaten food picked fresh from vines and trees, harvested from the earth, or hand slaughtered and cooked. Now imagine your body suddenly discovering instant soup, frozen dinner meals, candy bars, and Frappuccinos. These newer food inventions take more work and effort to process and digest, which can exhaust a key player in your digestive system— the liver. If the liver is overworked trying to manage lots of sugar, preservatives, food coloring, and the like, it is less likely to do its main job— getting rid of toxins that your body no longer needs and keeping your blood sugar balanced throughout the day. The good news is that with proper food choices, we can support a liver that happily cleans your blood thoroughly so toxins easily move out of your body.

Another important goal of eating well is elimination. Elimination of what? Well, I'm talking about poop. If you're not using the toilet daily, you will more than likely have backed-up trash in your body that needs clearing out. That trash might try to seep out as foul body odor or breath, or as acne and skin eruptions. None of the above helps you feel like your best self in private or public, so let's make sure the trash in our bodies is taken out daily. The other problem when we don't eliminate daily is that our hormonal trash can get backed up too and sent right back into our bloodstream, which throws other hormones out of whack.

WHEN NOT TO RECYCLE

While recycling is awesome for plastic bottles and metal cans, recycled hormones are quite the opposite. Remember estrogen, one of our hormone helpers? Estrogen can go a bit overboard and want to dominate all other hormones. We said earlier that estrogen helps you feel confident and capable. Well, too much can suppress other helpers that need their time to shine. When we don't have bowel movements every day, estrogen can keep stealing the spotlight, which may make the week before your period feel like an internal battle. Bloating, irritability, constipation, mood swings, and breast tenderness are often signs that estrogen has dominated the other helpers and is particularly overshadowing our inner chill chick, progesterone. Thankfully, food can be the best mediator in this scenario.

Because your design has the potential to create life, everything about your body is programmed to nurture a little human. This means that your body easily stores nutrients and adjusts how quickly or slowly you digest your food to ensure there's always enough fuel to create a healthy level of hormones in your body and potentially grow a baby if you become pregnant. This is also why your hormones get crazy when you don't feed yourself well. To know which foods make our hormones happiest, let's start with the foods that our hormones don't love so much and why we should limit them:

Trans-fatty acids: These fats start in one form but are transformed into another. Their altered state is not readily recognizable by your body, so sometimes your body doesn't know how to use them well. We find trans fats in most cooking oils, fried snacks, and margarine. Everyone, not just my fellow chemistry lovers, should know that trans fatty acids have hydrogen added to them to make them solid at room temperature, which restaurants and food companies love because it makes these fats easier to store, work with, and reuse. Trans fatty acids are a huge money maker for those who work with them but a health hazard for those who eat them.

Sugar: Who doesn't like sweets? Very few people for sure, but not all sweets are the same, and your body knows the difference between a food that is naturally sweet and artificially sweetened. When we enjoy the sweetness of a strawberry, sweet potato, or date, our body recognizes its origin and processes it accordingly. Added sweeteners like corn syrup, sugar, sucralose, aspartame, saccharin, and others are not as familiar to your body. They raise your blood sugar very quickly, which makes your liver work extra hard to bring your blood sugar levels down. This extra work can adjust your body's metabolism and gut bacteria, telling your body to store artificial sweeteners as belly fat.

For many reasons, it's great to limit the habit of adding sweeteners to your meals and drinking sweetened beverages in place of water. Sodas and fruit drinks might be tasty going down, but they can't hydrate your body like water does. Much like a plant needs water to absorb nutrients from the soil, our bodies need water to nourish our cells, bring nutrition and remove waste from them. Water, whole fruit, and coconut water are nature's best hydration sources. If you're not used to the taste of plain water, you can try adding a squeeze of lime or lemon, adding fresh fruit to water for a naturally infused flavor, or try filtered or spring water.

Factory-farmed meat and dairy: The sad truth is that a significant amount of food available in the developed world was very likely grown on a factory farm. Milk, cheese, yogurt, and meat are all sourced from animals. To make as many animal products as possible, factory farms often put way too many animals in too small of a space. When animals live in unnaturally close quarters, without the freedom to move freely and graze, they tend to get very sick. To prevent this, these animals are often given antibiotics— drugs that kill all kinds of bacteria.

To make the animals grow larger and produce more meat and milk, they are given artificial growth hormones. All of the drugs and hormones injected into the animals ultimately reach the plates of those who eat animals and their products. Antibiotics might be helpful when treating an infection, but when they are stirred into your milkshake or seasoning your steak, they can also destroy some of the good bacteria that your body needs to stay healthy. Growth hormones intended to plump up animals can be mistaken for your own body's hormones, which might make your body produce less of the healthy hormones you need. Additionally, growth hormones can impact how early you get your first period and how quickly your body develops.

I don't share this to coerce you to become vegetarian. But, I do want to encourage you to start thinking about your food choices and how they affect you. You might be too young to live on your own, but you're not too young to cook. You can also ask your parents or guardians to rethink the foods they eat and help them make healthier food choices for the entire family.

Processed Soy: Do you like mock meats? Vegan steaks, chick-un, or soy milk? I love them all but discovered some years ago that they don't love my hormones so much. Processed soy products contain phytoestrogens that can throw off the concentrations of natural estrogen that your body makes. If you choose to eat soy, your body will likely respond better to less processed forms like tofu, tempeh, miso, and natto. If you live in the Western hemisphere, make sure you choose organic soy products that are non-GMO (genetically modified organisms— a natural food ingredient was somehow changed by human engineering). Like trans fats, GMOs are essentially foreign substances that your body doesn't recognize and can't fully process. Be vigilant about observing how your body responds to soy and other foods listed here.

Our ethnic background and personal biology can also impact how food affects us, so be an investigator and discover for yourself which foods make your body feel most vibrant and balanced. If in your cultural heritage your family has eaten certain traditional foods for generations, your body might be well adapted to them. Whereas eating foods not traditionally eaten in your part of the world or your culture might not agree with your body right away. Aside from culture, we may have genes in our personal DNA that make certain foods easier or harder to digest, like intolerances to dairy, caffeine, gluten, etc.

Caffeine: Whether you're a coffee or a tea person, caffeine can be in either. Caffeine is a stimulant by nature that often excites you when you're feeling sluggish but also tends to create a stress response in the body. This can raise your stress levels and rob your body of the building blocks it needs to create healthy hormone levels. Try reducing your caffeine intake by opting for decaffeinated options (which means the caffeine is significantly less or removed), herbal teas (teas other than green, red, or black tea), and coffee alternatives. Anytime you have to rely on a specific product to help maintain your energy, there's a potential to develop an unhealthy dependency on that product. Dependency can easily turn into addiction, and teenagers have to carefully manage all of the new pleasure receptors that are developing in their brains. So be aware of your relationship with foods, beverages, habits, and relationships that make you feel like you can't survive without them (water would be an exception here, as well as wholesome foods).

Herbal teas are an amazing alternative to caffeinated beverages (especially sodas and energy drinks). Rather than robbing your body of nutrients, herbal teas can nourish you with vitamins and minerals while being refreshing.

WHAT KINDS OF FOODS DO HORMONES LOVE?

Seasonal fruits: Seasonal fruits offer your body essential vitamins and minerals, as well as hydration on a cellular level. Drinking water is important, but so is consuming fruits, which are like nature's perfectly balanced beverage. Colorful fruits, preferably organic or naturally grown, can make your hormones do the happy dance because they have a natural sweetness and fiber, which gently raises your blood sugar and gives you energy. If you're not sure how a fruit was grown, I would suggest soaking the fruits in a bowl of water with a splash of white vinegar or a dash of baking soda added to remove any chemicals from the surface. Alternatively, peeling the skin will remove questionable contaminant contact. Either way, try to enjoy several servings daily.

Vegetables: Colorful vegetables, just like fruits, deliver key vitamins to your body. Some vegetables that are especially loved by our bodies include cruciferous veggies like broccoli, cauliflower, kale, and Brussels sprouts. When cooked, these vegetables are loving to your liver and help you to process your hormones and eliminate them. Green leafy vegetables like spinach, chard, and bok choy are also nutritional powerhouses and, like many other veggies, are best digested when steamed, roasted, or otherwise cooked. Because we can't peel our greens, try to eat certified organic or naturally grown produce from local farmers. If you can, feel free to grow some of your own in your backyard, balcony, or windowsill.

If you've bought the lie that veggies are gross, then it's time to mature your taste buds and start exploring all of the diverse and delicious ways vegetables can be prepared. Boiling or microwaving frozen peas cannot compare to roasted cauliflower or Brussels sprouts, veggie stir-fries and curries, or rich and flavorful salads with different homemade sauces.
Here are some of my favorite homemade sauces to eat with veggies.

Tomato sauce: blend fresh tomatoes, onions, bell peppers, and garlic with herbs like oregano, thyme, marjoram, and basil.

Cashew cream: blend soaked raw cashews with nutritional yeast, garlic, lemon juice, sea salt, and olive oil.

Spicy peanut sauce: blend fresh ginger, garlic, lime juice, peanut butter, water, date or maple syrup, and sea salt

Healthy fats: Low-fat foods were once a popular trend, but there is now a greater awareness of how important fats are in our diet. Fats are the fuel that our liver uses to make cholesterol and build some of our key hormone helpers like estrogen, progesterone, and testosterone. However, all fats are not created equal, so eating healthy sources of fats is really important. Some of the healthiest fats are found in foods like avocados, olives, sesame seeds, and nuts. They can also come from animal-sourced fats like ghee, cheese, tallow, and butter made from grass-fed animals. Not only does your body need fat to build hormones, but fats will also help keep your skin clear, supple, and glowing, and help you have regular bowel movements too.

Protein: At every meal, our body needs protein. Protein is a combination of amino acids that helps our cells complete essential functions. Athletes tend to focus a lot of attention on how much protein they eat because it builds and repairs tissues and muscles. We should all make sure that we have enough protein in our diet because it also helps to keep our blood sugar stable and makes us feel full after a meal. As we mentioned before, if you have access to locally and naturally grown animal products, they are generally free of the added hormones and chemicals given to animals grown in factory farms.

Similarly, we can find good sources of protein in beans, lentils, cheese, eggs, whole grains, nuts, and seeds. Vegetables and fruits also contain protein but in very small amounts. How much protein you should eat daily depends on your lifestyle, body size, and age. If you're still hungry after eating a meal or craving something sweet right away, try adding more protein and healthy fats to your meal and observe the difference. Adding eggs or cheese, a few tablespoons of nut butter or seeds, an extra handful of beans or quinoa, or a portion of meat can help to round out a meal that isn't keeping you full.

Herbs: Plant medicine is a great ally to the menstruating body. In each phase of our menstrual cycle, there are wonderful herbs that we can incorporate as teas into our daily routine. Some herbs, like nettle or moringa, are a great source of iron and can be really helpful after your period. Dandelion and turmeric are very cleansing and can help your liver get rid of high estrogen levels from your ovulatory phase. Holy basil or ashwagandha are great herbs for adapting to stress, which tends to be slightly higher in your luteal phase.

Hibiscus, ginger, and cinnamon tea help increase your circulation while on your period, and chamomile relaxes muscle cramps.

Herbal tea is a great substitute for caffeinated drinks, but not all herbs taste the same. Some taste earthy or bitter, while others are fragrant or sweet. Some are spicy and heating, while others are cooling and calming. Herbal teas can be enjoyed iced or hot with honey and lemon if you haven't gotten used to their natural taste yet. Give these amazing plants a chance to be a part of your life.

TO GO VEG OR NOT

In the Introduction, I told you about my vegan friend from college. Her name is Sarah and she was the president of our campus' Environmental Committee and a huge vegan advocate. When she introduced herself to me as a vegan, I had no clue what that meant. As a Jamaican, I regularly interacted with vegetarians from adjacent Seventh-Day Adventist and Rastafarian communities. I knew diets could be connected to personal ethics around health and spiritual understandings about what it means to be or have a healthy 'temple' or body. However, Sarah was the first person I knew who didn't eat animals because of how they were treated. Images of caged chickens and tortured cows compelled me to ask Chef James to hold the beef in my nightly pasta at the university cafeteria.

I personally felt so much healthier and lighter when I gave up eating meat. As I shared earlier, my period was no longer painful, heavy, or difficult. To me, that was the only evidence I needed to stick with my meat-free life. But, my periods were still very irregular and in my late 20s and early 30s, I had difficulty getting and staying pregnant. I can't say for sure that my vegan lifestyle was to blame, but I do question whether my body was receiving everything it needed to maintain a healthy period and meet the demands of growing, birthing, and breastfeeding a baby while not depleting my energy and nutrient reserves.

As you explore different dietary options and lifestyle choices, I ask that you always think of your period. In Chapter 6, I described what a holistically balanced period looks like. Let that be your compass as you move forward and be curious. How does your period respond to the removal or addition of certain foods? How do your hormonal symptoms improve or worsen when the way you eat shifts? Consider that there are universal nutritional needs, but your personal constitution needs to be considered when evaluating what works best for you.

I value the lives of animals and agree with data that illustrates meat is generally overconsumed at a rate that our planet cannot sustain. I also believe that taking an animal's life should not be taken lightly and, if done, must be handled with great reverence, integrity, and care for the sanctity of life. If you choose to eat a plant-based diet, this also must be handled with great reverence, integrity, and care for the sanctity of your life, the planet, and other living beings. I'm not in a position to make prescriptions for your health, but I do encourage you to be more committed to your wellness than the identity politics of labels.

CHAPTER RECAP:

- The foods we eat can help or hurt our hormones.
- Spending time preparing and planning meals can help us achieve peaceful periods.
- Inflammatory foods create stress in our bodies, but there are many tasty substitutes.

Journal Prompt:
Pick three hormone-friendly foods from this chapter. Look up recipes that you want to try cooking using them.

CHAPTER 10:
SHOULD I WORK OUT OR CHILL OUT?

Being able to move our bodies is a true blessing. It reminds us that we are very much alive and gets the blood flowing to every part of our being. Our bloodstream is the river that delivers nourishment to our cells and removes the wastes we no longer need. When we exercise, that river flows stronger, and everything moves in and out more effectively. Physical activity also flushes our main stress hormone, cortisol, out of our bodies. So, when you feel overwhelmed or under a great deal of pressure, think of ways to actually move that stress out of your body.

Sometimes our bodies hold memories of difficult feelings or experiences that can be remembered or re-experienced at various times. Movement, touch, breathing practices, and your awareness of sensations in the body are examples of somatic practices that can help your nervous system find safety in the present moment, instead of reliving a challenging moment from the past. This will help your brain to know that you are not under long-term stress, so it won't go into survival mode and shut down some of the activities that help you thrive, like ovulating and menstruating.

Have you ever missed a period and wondered why? Was it an especially stressful time in your life? This is what stress does. It can tell your body to focus on your essential life functions like breathing, digesting, and staying alive. Even though having a period is a critical part of being healthy, it is not considered an essential life function. So, in times of stress or difficulty, your body has no problem quitting your period to focus on other tasks.

WHEN TO PAUSE

Another critical movement our body needs is no movement at all— rest. Sleeping is important for happy hormones and a healthy period. It deeply recharges your body, cleanses your blood, and clears your brain— all of which help ensure your body has the energy it needs to do its best work. It is optimal to be asleep by 10:00 PM, so all parts of your body can get the rest they need to function best. Your liver has an important job to do every night after 10:00 PM— it scrubs your entire bloodstream clean of toxins. Staying up late and, even worse, eating very late at night can tire your liver at a time when it would much rather focus on its work.

Remember, your circadian rhythm is the daily internal clock that tells you when to wake up and rest. By forcing your body to stay up late with caffeine and energy drinks, we confuse that clock and its natural order. It's hard enough falling asleep as a teenager because melatonin, the hormone that helps usher you into dreamland, tends to be produced later at night than for children and adults. Occasionally, we might desire or need to stay up late, but if we follow our circadian clock most days of the week, our bodies can better handle the occasional late night without disrupting our overall energy too much.

Moving according to our infradian rhythm or our monthly hormonal clock is just as important as our daily circadian rhythm. There are times when our hormones benefit from us being up and active, as well as slowing down and resting. Can you guess which time of the month your body needs to definitely be resting and not moving too fast or too hard? Hint: It's a time when your body is releasing, and you might find your energy declining or turning inward.

When you menstruate, your body releases the tissue in your uterus that it built up in the month. With blood as the liquid and your vessels as the faucet, your body cleanses your womb, which is a lot of work. If you don't take the time to slow down, your period can last for more days than necessary. Having your period doesn't mean that you can't exercise at all. It means it's best to slow down your movements with scenic walks, deep stretches, and yoga- not running, jumping, doing cartwheels, and being super active and all over the place. Excessive sweat can drain your body of energy and nutrients that it's already using to manage menstruation. Lots of cardio activity can encourage your body to bleed even more, so embrace the time to rest and get recharged for the weeks ahead.

> **Did you know?** Women account for 39% of participants in exercise studies and when females are included in sports and exercise research, it is only during the first half of the menstrual cycle, when hormone levels are low, or when using hormonal birth control.

WHEN TO TURN IT UP

When we find our natural energy rising after our period, it's a great time to find enjoyable ways to be active. Whether you like to dance, run, lift, or flip, being active can help use your energy and eliminate the hormones that you no longer need. Your body is burning energy a little slower than usual, so exercise can help you feel energized. Ovulation is when your energy peaks, so if you have big feats to tackle, like mountain biking, a challenging trek, or a marathon, this is your time to shine and witness your prime physical performance!

At some point in the month, you might find intense exercises more tiring than before or it's harder to get up in the morning. Once you've ovulated, those potent hormones that make you feel pumped and energized start to dip and another set of hormones brings your focus toward preparation, organizing, and finishing your projects. This is a great time to focus on strength training instead of cardio or heart-pumping exercises. Building strength can be done through weight lifting or pilates, but don't break too much of a sweat in the days leading up to your period.

Is there such a thing as too much exercise? Absolutely! Exercising too much at the wrong time of the month can increase stress in your body instead of relieving it. During your luteal (or inner fall) phase, your cortisol levels are naturally higher, while your blood sugar is naturally lower. By overexerting yourself at this time with high-intensity exercise, instead of building muscle and burning fat, your body can break down your muscles and store fat. You can effectively empty your gas tank with little to run on for the hormonal ride ahead. Again, the goal is to work smarter, not harder. You don't need to run for miles every day to be healthy, but you do need to protect your hormones and honor your body's need to both move and rest to be healthy.

The goal of exercising should never be about how you look, but rather how you feel. I meet many women who tell me they are healthy— they exercise and eat salads daily, drink smoothies and celery juice, but their period is super painful, irregular, or absent. Your period is a powerful guide and can tell you when you're doing too much or not enough for your body to feel its best. A healthy, pain-free period should only last about four days, with fresh red blood, no clotting, and no cramping. It ideally arrives once every 28-30 days consistently and should not cause crazy symptoms that disrupt your life and peace of mind. By moving our body for health's sake, not size's sake, we make sure that our movement serves us, not sabotages us.

CHAPTER RECAP:

- Movement and rest are equally important for peaceful periods.
- Exercise is a great way to release stress and encourage a healthy lifestyle.
- Rest and gentle exercise are most helpful during our period.

Journal Prompt:
Describe your favorite way to move your body. How and where do you like to move?

CHAPTER 11:
HOW DO I KNOW WHEN MY PERIOD IS COMING?

We can't start to make peace with our period until we begin to really understand it. Our periods unmistakably show up with a menstrual flow, but we can 'honor' our monthly guest by preparing for its arrival. Perhaps you're thinking, how will preparing for my period change anything? Considering the hormonal and physical changes that happen when we menstruate, we can adjust our schedules, meals, and habits to make our transition to bleeding a lot smoother.

Keeping Track
Tracking your period is an important practice. Knowing how often your period comes is a critical part of identifying your regular cycle length and a key piece of information about your hormonal health. Every 29 days is a healthy average number of days between periods, counting Day 1 of your period as the first day of menstrual flow that requires using a period product. Teen periods can be a bit irregular in the first few years of menstruation. Tracking is an immensely helpful tool to get familiar with how your body is adjusting to your monthly rhythm. Using a paper calendar or app, you can note the date when your period starts each month and how long it lasts. There are even free period tracking apps, but do your research, as some apps profit from sharing and selling your personal information.

Check Your Charts
If you suspect you have some major hormonal problems, like absent periods or intense symptoms, it would be helpful to know more information about your period by charting. Charting is the process of documenting your daily waking temperature (known as your basal body temperature) as well as noting your cervical mucus or vaginal discharge and other symptoms. Everything from skin breakouts to migraines or bloating can have a cyclical pattern which is hard to notice without taking notes. Observing what your body is doing gains deep insights into when and why your symptoms are occurring. Instead of isolating your experiences, you can connect them to the bigger story your body is telling you and respond more helpfully.

To start charting, you'll need a basal body thermometer. It's similar to other thermometers, but it's more precise and can report your temperature within two decimal places. Next, you'll need charting paper (see Resource Hub for downloadable charts). Every morning, before rising out of bed, you'll need to grab your basal body thermometer and place it in your mouth. Make sure your thermometer is within arm's reach from the night before. Close your lips around the thermometer to begin measuring it. You need to have rested for at least five hours to produce an accurate reading, and it's best if you take the temperature at around the same time each day. A digital basal body thermometer will beep or alert when the reading is complete, which can take one to two minutes. If you can, wait five to ten minutes for a more accurate reading. Record your temperature and mark it on your chart.

Get More Data

In addition to your temperature, you also want to make notes about your cervical mucus throughout the day. When you use the bathroom, notice if your cervical mucus is present or absent, sticky or slippery, clear or opaque, and add that to your chart. As you get closer to the middle of your menstrual cycle, you should notice more slippery, clear cervical mucus just before a noticeable jump in temperature. If the jump is about 0.4 degrees Fahrenheit or 0.2 degrees Celsius, observe if it remains higher for a few days. If it does, that means you've ovulated! If you go from one period to the next without noticing a jump in temperature, you might not have ovulated that month. Keep charting and consider working with a Fertility Awareness Method (FAM) Educator to check your charts and help you better understand them.

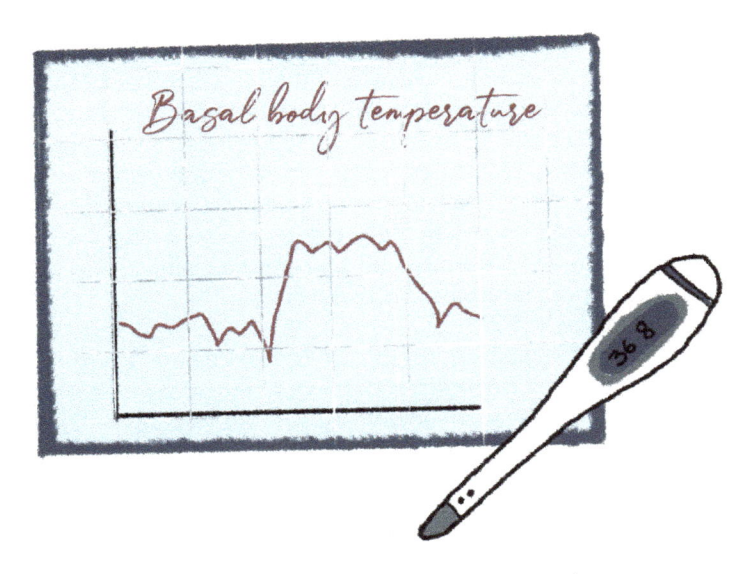

Charting allows you to recognize if and when you're ovulating, so you will know when to expect your menstrual flow. The length of your luteal phase will be fairly constant every month, so once you've confirmed ovulation, you can count the days leading up to your period, and plan your life accordingly. This awareness can make living life in your beautiful body so much easier! While it is common for school and family life to dictate how most of our life operates, we can focus on the activities we can control and plan them when our bodies and minds are most available for them.

Go Inward
Journaling is a fun way to explore your inner workings and how they are impacted by your menstrual cycle. Some people experience vivid dreams while menstruating or have moments of tremendous creativity and

inspiration, as well as doubt and negative self-talk. Writing down these subtle and not-so-subtle feelings and thoughts can help you realize the full cycle of your energy and mental activities. Remember estrogen, one of our hormone helpers? When it rises, we feel fearless, social, and capable of moving mountains. Our other helper, progesterone, reigns us in after we ovulate to reflect, contemplate, and be a bit more protective and cautious. Both work together to ensure that we don't burn out from the brilliance of our peak energy and visions nor do we become overly critical of ourselves and others without tangible actions and tasks.

Menstruation is a built-in season of retreat, where warmth, rest, and comfort should feel inviting and soothing. A retreat can be a powerful time of insight and rejuvenation, unearthing wisdom to carry with us when we emerge. Writing down what you experience during your cycle phases can help you accept the ebbs and flow of your energy and thought patterns while capturing gems to take with you throughout the other phases of your cycle. Syncing your life with your cycle is boss-level status and will ultimately depend on how much autonomy you have over your daily schedule, meal selections, and activities. The idea of synchronizing how you move and function concerning your menstrual cycle has proven to be a powerful biohacking tool for menstruating folks. Any kind of hack is a smarter and more efficient way of doing something. Cycle syncing may sound complicated, but like everything else, it can be learned with patience and practice.

Level Up

Cycle syncing means specifically scheduling certain habits and activities for specific phases of the month. So, for example, if we know that we can expect our available energy to be lowest when we menstruate, we can scale back on activities that require a lot of physical exertion, like dance practice, hosting a party, or giving a major presentation. On the other hand, if we know that our ovulatory phase is when our energy levels peak, we can plan intense hikes, social outings, or big events at that time. As for food, menstruation is a time of flow or circulation. We help our blood circulate freely in the body by eating warm foods and drinking warm beverages. This is a time when avoiding icy, cold, or frozen foods and drinks would be best to prevent unnecessary clotting or cramping during our period.

Take a closer look at *Chapter 5: "Why Do I Feel So Different Every Week?"* and think of practical ways to incorporate some cycle awareness into your lifestyle. Letting your parents or guardians know what you're up to can help rally support for the changes you want to make. That might also mean you need to step up your organizational and culinary skills if your parents or guardians are not sure what you want to try out and how it will work. Helping with activity scheduling, meal planning, and food preparation can be an easy way to get support for your hormone-friendly way of living.

CHAPTER RECAP:

- Using calendars, journals, or apps to track our period can help us notice symptom patterns.
- By charting our basal body temperature, we can know when we've ovulated and when to expect our next period.
- Being aware of our menstrual phases helps us to plan our meals and activities in helpful ways.

Journal Prompt:
If you know when to expect your period, how would you prepare? What would you do the week before your period? What about the day before your period?

CHAPTER 12:
CAN PERIOD POWER CHANGE THE WORLD?

If your current lifestyle is much different from the advice I've laid out here for you, you might be feeling overwhelmed. Maybe every meal you eat comes from a microwavable package, or the stove is rarely turned on in your home. Maybe you can't recall the last time you've had fresh fruit, fallen asleep before midnight, or broke a sweat. Everyone has a first step that we can take. We can begin by focusing on one new habit that we're willing to try or one old habit we want to move away from. But why? Why even start, and what do you have to gain?

Love, you are an amazing human being with limitless potential. Your passions and skills bring meaning to life and impact the world around you. When you are no longer tugged and pulled by the rocky rollercoaster of hormonal symptoms, your mind and heart are free to do things you love. No pain to plow through, no cramps to slow you down, no mood swings to make you feel crazy. You can surf on the tide of your hormones instead of feeling drowned by them and thrashing in the waves.

Perhaps reaching for pain medication has been your coping tool, or you depend on birth control to suppress your period and certain symptoms. But guess what? Food is your medicine, and wellness is your most powerful winning strategy. You can be well, whole, and balanced. And when you learn to give yourself the care you deserve, you can feel better, treat others better, and teach others how to treat you better too.

Having a menstrual cycle is an incredible gift, though many societies make it feel like a deficiency. Women are not smaller or weaker versions of men. In our own right, we are the creators of a life worth living. Our creativity and intuition, our empathy and problem-solving skills— we bring life to living and beauty to form. By embracing our design instead of silencing or suppressing it, we can allow our gifts to fully bloom and beautify the world around us.

Green Your Period

Another powerful way our attitudes about our period can impact the world is our choice of menstrual care products. In some parts of the world, disposable menstrual pads are not affordable, so women use cloth and some unsuitable substitutes to fill the gap. But, even in the developed world, more folks are reexamining their use of disposable pads in favor of organic and/or natural disposable pads, reusable cloth pads, or period panties.

> **Did you know?** Most of us menstruate for about four decades. That's roughly 480 periods in our lifetimes. Stanford Magazine published that in the United States alone, an estimated 12 billion pads and 7 million tampons are thrown out each year. And because conventional sanitary pads are made of up to 90% plastic, they will still be around for another 500-800 years.

WHAT PERIOD PRODUCT SHOULD YOU USE AND WHEN?

Disposable pads are honestly the most convenient, without a doubt, but the trash they make isn't convenient at all. Plastic in disposable pads will remain on the planet longer than you or I because it is not biodegradable, which means that it can't easily break down and become soil material. Additionally, if the cotton used is bleached white, the bleaching chemicals can irritate your vulva. Healthier and more environmentally friendly alternatives include unbleached, plastic-free, organic cotton pads. Wielding your purchasing power gives you peace of mind, knowing your monthly bleed isn't creating permanent pollution on the planet.

Period panties are pretty cool in that they look like plain underwear and can be washed and reused. These special underwear are a leak-free option that can hold your flow without soiling your clothes. In the same way that you change your pad throughout the day, you would change your period panties which can be soaked or rinsed in cold water and later washed in your washing machine or by hand. The unsuspecting briefs are not unusually bulky, nor do they have "PERIOD PANTIES" written in huge letters all over them. They are discreet, functional, and come in many styles and colors.

Reusable cloth pads can work with any kind of underwear and can be changed throughout the day, just like any other period product. However, you don't just throw them in the trash. You need to carry a waterproof bag if you're changing a reusable cloth pad outside the home. When you return home, you'll have the option of rinsing or soaking the pads in cold water before machine washing them. What's most important for reusable cloth products is that they must be thoroughly dry before reuse. Line drying in the sun is a great way to brighten stains and eliminate any residual odors; however, a drying machine can dry them thoroughly too.

Menstrual cups are small flexible cups that hold your period blood inside your body. The base of the cup sits near your vaginal opening, while the 'bowl' of the cup sits inside your vaginal canal. Menstrual cups can be very helpful when you can't throw away disposable pads or can't wash reusable pads or period panties. Also, they last for about ten years, so it's a very cheap way to manage your period. Although menstrual cups are made of soft silicone or latex rubber, some find it awkward to insert a folded cup into their body.

Perhaps the sound of a reusable period product sounds gross, but hear me out: in most supermarkets, the only period products available are typical pads- bleached cotton, absorbent fibers wrapped in plastic, and scented with perfumes. The chemicals of all these components, though worn outside of your vulva, can affect the delicate tissues of your vagina. Vaginal tissues are easily irritated by unnatural chemicals, which can create dryness, burning, itching, or heavier bleeding. By switching to non-toxic pads, many notice less period pain, bleeding, and irritation.

Before You Plug
Tampons are not a preferred period product. Leaving a tampon in your vagina for too long (more than eight hours) can cause health problems and prevent the natural downward flow of blood out of your body. As a result, plugging the vaginal canal with a period product might create cramping or discomfort. Some find this to be true with menstrual cups as well. Regardless of what period products you use, make sure reusable products are washed and dried thoroughly before use. Also, wash your hands before

handling anything that comes into contact with your precious vulva. Your private parts are sensitive, so handle them with care.

When we choose sustainable ways of handling our period, we choose our health, the planet, and its well-being. Tapping into your period power makes the world a better place, both inwardly and outwardly.

CHAPTER RECAP:

- Our period experience can affect our self-esteem, relationships, and environments.
- Choosing reusable or biodegradable period care products reduces plastic pollution and waste.
- Having a peaceful period can help you experience the full benefit of menstruation without significant disruption or discomfort every month.

Journal Prompt:
Draw the life cycle of a period product that you use. Where did it originate? How was it grown or manufactured? What will happen after it is no longer in use?

CHAPTER 13:
WHAT IF I DON'T HAVE A PERIOD?

More than likely, you had or will have your first period between the ages of 11 and 13, but for some, it will be much earlier or later. The age of menarche or your first period can be impacted by family genetics, diet, body weight, lifestyle, and how well some of your key organs are working.

If you're 14 years old and haven't had a period yet, there are several ways you can support your body to nudge the first bleed to begin. First, we need to make sure you're eating enough food and have enough body fat. If your body perceives that you are not well-fed or have too little body fat, then ovulating won't be seen as a priority next to other functions like breathing, digesting, moving, thinking, etc. This is especially important for athletes or fitness enthusiasts who often experience disrupted or delayed periods because of intense exercise and training, low body fat, or not eating enough to sustain their physical demands. Similarly, psychological and physical stress gives your body the message that you are unsafe and no energy is available for ovulating. This can be true in cases of extreme stress, chronic illness, rapid weight loss, etc.

Increasing your calories, especially healthy fats, tells our bodies that we are safe and healthy. Regular meals further communicate that we have regular access to food. Eating three meals throughout the day and snacking when you feel hungry in between is not excessive and might be just what your body needs to bring your period online. Teen athletes, in particular, need enough nourishment to support their growing bodies and hormone production, as well as to fuel the physical demands of training and performing.

Fickle with Food?
If you're having a difficult relationship with food or think you might have some disordered eating habits, consider talking to a therapist who specializes in this area and can help you unravel thoughts or beliefs about food or your body that aren't serving your health. Health and beauty encompass many shapes, sizes, and forms, so be mindful of any messages

that tell you otherwise. Also, be wary of diets encouraging you to overly restrict or eliminate carbohydrates or fats. Menstruating bodies have many nutritional needs that need to be met with a variety of wholesome, delicious foods that you enjoy eating.

Mind Your Meds

Certain medications, like hormonal birth control, antidepressants, chemotherapy, antipsychotics, and antibiotics, can also chase away your periods. If your period is missing for more than three to six months, contact a medical professional who is open to supporting your health without dismissing your biological need for a monthly period. Some doctors say periods only matter if you want a baby, but current science tells us that regular ovulation sets a foundation for robust health for many years to come and reduces our likelihood of long-term diseases.

Stress Overload

Life stressors can rock our world and put a pause on our period too. Family changes like divorce or separation, losing a loved one, moving to a new city, or drastic shifts in key relationships can create a lot of stress. If we aren't careful, that stress can put our bodies into a survival mode where we operate on the most basic level— not flourishing as our fully fertile selves. Stress management techniques like deep breathing, meditation, physical fitness, saunas, creative expression, dance, play, laughter, and therapy can help reduce our cortisol (stress hormone) levels.

When our bodies experience sustained stress over long periods, some hormones step in to help shoulder the load. Progesterone, for example, can be borrowed in times of high stress, which means we have less of it available to keep our estrogen levels balanced. Be sure to make a regular practice of something relaxing and joyful every day, even if it's just a moment to gaze at a stunning sunrise or hug someone you love.

Micros

There are some key nutrients that our bodies need for ovulation, such as iodine, selenium, zinc, iron, magnesium, and Vitamin A. Some key sources of these nutrients are sea vegetables, shellfish, Brazil nuts, beans, eggs, etc.

Not having enough of these essential elements can make it challenging for our bodies to have monthly periods. After paying attention to what you're eating and how often, exercise intensity, and stress management, you might also want to speak to a medical practitioner about checking some of your vitamin and mineral levels to make sure your body has what it needs to bring your period back into the picture.

CHAPTER RECAP:

- A missing period can tell us that our body's nutritional needs aren't being met or the body is under too much physical or emotional stress.
- Regular meals with enough carbohydrates and fats tell our bodies we are safe enough to ovulate.
- We need key nutrients to maintain a regular period every month.

Journal Prompt:

Has your period ever gone missing?

What's the longest length of time you went without a period?

In what ways can you support your body if your period goes absent?

CONCLUSION

Now that you've reached the end of this book, it's time to let you in on my little secret— this book isn't just for teens. It's for mothers like myself, who hadn't learned what a healthy period was until they were in their 30s (or later). It's for grandmothers, like my mom, who were never taught to see periods as worthy of celebration. This book is even for my 95-year-old grandmother, and I'll tell you why.

Last year, while on the phone with my grandma, I told her that I was teaching a period class to my daughter and her friends so they would be prepared for their first period and know how to care for themselves every month, just as I've taught you in this book. We were learning about how different cultures recognized and honored menstruation. My grandma paused. For her, growing up in the countryside of Jamaica, her first period was not even acknowledged.

As the daughter of a Chinese immigrant, my grandmother spent most of her childhood behind the counter of a country store where neighbors would buy sugar, flour, butter, and salted mackerel on credit. Neither her father nor her half-Scottish mother prepared her for her period. But my grandmother was an avid reader, so she already knew what to expect. At the age of 14, she recognized that her period had begun and grabbed a yardstick to knock down a box of disposable pads from the top shelf. Every month, she would fasten these pads into her underwear and dispose of them in a pit latrine (outdoor toilet) in the yard. Every month, from her first period to her last, she bled without a trace of her personal rhythm. No one held her hand, ushering her through the rite of passage into womanhood and showing her the way.

I explained to my grandmother that periods are special and shape the way we feel in and about our bodies. At this point she told me, "Your daughter is very lucky to have you." My grandmother can find peace in the fact that though she faced her period alone, concealed from everyone, her great-granddaughter doesn't have to do the same.

I especially wrote this book for my children. They gave me the opportunity to practice talking about periods in a natural way that wasn't weird or uncomfortable. I grew confident enough to explain to them when I was on my period (or moon cycle, womb cleanse, monthly retreat, or whatever more interesting way you want to describe a period) and they noticed my different habits on those days. Both my daughter and son grew up watching me wrap my hips, slow down, make fresh ginger tea, and rest deeply while menstruating. They loved sitting at my feet during womb steaming sessions before and after my period, curiously asking what the steam felt like.

The groundwork for this book came through my work as a peristeam facilitator and holistic menstrual health educator. Working with private clients and teaching courses, I recognized exactly what Dr. Laurena mentioned in the foreword of this book— reproductive health issues are rooted in menstrual dysfunction. Most adult women are desperate for answers and solutions once their disruptive symptoms can no longer be ignored. But what if we knew how to have healthy periods before they even start? What if we could be introduced to menstruation through a lens of seeing purpose, power, and awe in our design? What if we could bypass decades of suffering and just protect the health of our period from the beginning? These are the inquiries that compelled me to write this book.

How to teach youth about periods was refined through workshops and small group classes I taught to pre-teens and teens to prepare for and support positive and peaceful periods. As a result, my daughter and her peers are living in a totally different reality than my peers and I lived in. Instead of feeling ignorance, shame, and trauma about their periods, they feel ready, equipped, and informed about what to expect. They know not to accept painful periods as normal and are genuinely excited to receive their monthly periods. They feel comfortable asking questions, checking their cervical mucus, washing reusable period care products, making teas, wrapping their wombs, and trying womb steaming. We are co-creating a new period culture.

While in the last stages of writing this book, my husband and I took our children to sight the new moon of Ramadan (the ninth lunar month of the Islamic calendar) with a few of our friends. All of our children, ages 3 to 12, studied the night sky scanning for the faint crescent until suddenly, all at once, they began to jump and yell. "I see it! I see it! It's over there! I see the new moon!". Their joy was contagious as they were all giddy and bouncing.

In that moment, a clear vision came to me— this is how I want every first period to be received. Everyone should feel joy, excitement, and anticipation. There shouldn't be shock or shame but rather a felt sense of true celebration, marking that something special, sacred, and beautiful has begun. This is how the book cover illustration came to be.

And lastly, the other person I wrote this book for is **you**. I want you to know, whether you menstruate or not, that periods are powerful. They do not make us weak or inferior to others. They should not be a source of disgust or embarrassment, but rather honor and sanctity. Periods can be peaceful, and this is my prayer for every menstruating person that you know.

We no longer have to pop pills and plug ourselves with tampons to "just bleed and carry on." We can pause. We can rest. We can honor our wombs. We can honor life. Let's choose this for ourselves and make space for others to do the same– in our homes, schools, workplaces, and communities. Let's end period poverty (thank you for doing your part by buying this book). Let's stop the period shame for good. Period.

GLOSSARY

A2 Milk: sourced from cow breeds that produce a specific protein that may be easier to digest

Acidic: having the properties of an acid, which is sour or sharp in taste with a pH below 7

Antidepressant: medication used to relieve or prevent persistent sadness and a lack of interest or pleasure in previously rewarding or enjoyable activities

Anti-inflammatory: medication used to prevent or reduce the extent to which your body's tissues respond to harmful stimuli

Antibiotics: medication used to treat or prevent infections by killing or inhibiting the growth of bacteria in or on the body, that is administered orally, topically, or by injection

Antipsychotic: medication used especially to manage symptoms like delusions, hallucinations, disordered thoughts, paranoia, etc.

Aspartame: an artificial sugar substitute used in foods and beverages

Assessment: the action or an instance of making a judgment about something

Auto-immunity: when the immune system attacks the body's own cells

Bacteria: a large group of single-cell microorganisms. Some cause infections and disease in animals and humans

Basal body temperature: the temperature of the body at rest, which is typically taken immediately after waking from sleep

Bias: a tendency to favor or oppose someone or something based on personal feelings and beliefs, not facts or reason

Biodegradable: the ability to be broken down into its base elements by microorganisms and the passage of time

Biohacking: using science and technology to make the body function better and more efficiently

Biology: a branch of knowledge that deals with living organisms and vital processes

Bloating: to cause abdominal swelling, usually by air (gas) or water

Blood clots: a thick and sticky clump of dried blood that stops blood from flowing through blood vessels

Blue light: light emitted from electronic device screens which mimics sunlight and can arouse the brain when it is normally time to rest

Bowel movement: an act of passing usually solid waste through the rectum and anus

Burnout: exhaustion of physical or emotional strength or motivation usually as a result of prolonged stress or frustration

Caffeine: a natural stimulant that increases the activity of the brain and nervous system

Cancer: abnormal cell growth with the potential to invade or spread to other parts of the body

Cardiac: relating to, situated near, or acting on the heart

Celsius: referring to measurements on the scale of temperature at which water freezes at 0° and boils at 100° under standard conditions

Cervical mucus: a fluid produced by and released from the cervix (opening of the uterus) often used to indicate when someone is most fertile

Chemotherapy: the therapeutic use of chemical agents to treat disease

Circadian rhythm: physical, mental, and behavioral changes that follow a 24-hour cycle, responding primarily to light and dark, and affecting most living things

Cisgender: identifying with the gender assigned at birth

Clots: a roundish thick lump usually formed by coagulation of a portion of liquid

Constipation: abnormally delayed or infrequent passage of usually dry, hardened feces

Constitution: physical makeup of an individual

Corpus luteum: a yellowish mass of progesterone-secreting endocrine tissue that forms immediately after ovulation

Cortisol: a hormone that regulates stress response, metabolism, and many other functions

Decaffeinated: having the caffeine removed, such as in soda or coffee

Deficiency: an amount that is lacking or inadequate

Dehydration: the physical state caused by not drinking enough fluid or by losing more fluid than is taken in

Diabetes: a disease in which the body's ability to produce or respond to the hormone insulin is impaired

Diagnosis: the art or act of identifying a disease from its signs and symptoms

Discharge: a fluid or mucus that exits the body

Disposable: designed to be used once or only a limited number of times and then thrown away

Douching: forcing a stream of liquid into the vagina

Elimination: the act of discharging or excreting waste products from the body

Endocrine system: several glands located across the body that create and release hormones

Endocrine-disrupting chemicals: natural or human-made chemicals that may mimic, block, or interfere with the body's hormones

Endometriosis: a painful condition where tissue like the uterine lining grows outside of the womb

Enhancers: an additive used to improve the flavor of food

Enzymes: proteins that speed up chemical reactions

Estrogen: a hormone associated with the female reproductive organs

Exhaustion: a feeling of constant tiredness or weakness that can be physical, mental, or a combination of both

Factory-farmed: a system of farming where a large number of animals are kept in a small closed area to maximize profit

Fahrenheit: referring to measurements on the scale of temperature at which water freezes at 32° and boils at 212° under standard conditions

Fatigue: weariness or exhaustion from labor, exertion, or stress

Fertility Awareness Method (FAM): natural ways to avoid or achieve pregnancy by tracking indicators, like basal body temperature, cervical mucus, and cervical position

Fertilization: the process of union between an egg and sperm by which a new individual is created

Fibroids: abnormal growths that develop in or on the uterus

Gallstones: hardened deposits of digestive fluid that can form in the gallbladder

Gelatinous: having the consistency of jelly or gel

Gene: a unit of inherited information that impacts how we develop

Genetic: of, relating to, caused by, or controlled by genes

Ghosting: the act or practice of abruptly cutting off all contact with someone usually without explanation

Glamorize: the act of making something seem more attractive or exciting than it is

GPS: global positioning system

Grind: persevering when doing something difficult or performing repetitive tasks to achieve a certain goal

Hangry: irritable or angry because of hunger

Heritage: something transmitted by or acquired from a predecessor

Hibernation: to be or become inactive or dormant

Hormones: chemical messengers that regulate vital processes in the body

Hustle: to urge forward with careless speed, often referring to the societal pressure to work oneself to extremes

Illumination: spiritual or intellectual enlightenment

Inadequate: not enough or insufficient

Infection: invasion and multiplication of harmful microorganisms in the body

Infradian rhythm: a bodily cycle that exceeds the circadian rhythm or daily cycle

Insulin: a hormone that lowers the amount of glucose in blood

Intricate: complex and having many elements

Intuition: the ability to understand something instinctively without the need for conscious reasoning

Irritation: inflammation or other discomfort in a body part caused by reaction to an irritating substance

Ligaments: fibrous connective tissues that connect bones to other bones or support an organ in place

Mass production: production of goods in considerable quantities usually by machinery

Meditation: a practice intended to train attention to awareness and produce a mentally clear and emotionally calm and stable state

Melatonin: a hormone made in the body to regulate sleep and wake cycles

Menarche: the first menstrual bleeding

Menopause: the natural ending of menstruation that usually occurs between the ages of 45 and 55 years old

Menorrhagia: menstrual bleeding that lasts more than seven days or is very heavy

Menstruation: monthly shedding of uterine lining or uterine cleanse

Metabolism: the set of life-sustaining chemical reactions mainly connected to deriving energy from food, converting food to building blocks, and eliminating metabolic wastes

Natural: not made or caused by humankind

Non-toxic: not containing poison or substances harmful to your health

Nourishment: the food necessary for growth, health, and good condition

Oocyte: egg cell

Organic: produced without artificial chemicals

Osteoporosis: a condition that develops when bone mineral density and bone mass decreases

Ovulation: a phase of the female menstrual cycle that involves the release of an egg (ovum) from one of the ovaries

Painkiller: something (such as a drug) that relieves pain

Pasteurize: a process of food preservation in which packaged and non-packaged foods (such as milk and fruit juices) are treated with mild heat to eliminate pathogens and extend shelf life

PCOS: see Polycystic Ovarian Syndrome

Peristeam hydrotherapy: exposing the perineum and pelvic area of the body to herbal steam as a form of support or treatment

Phytoestrogens: a chemical compound that occurs naturally in plants and has estrogen-like properties

Pituitary gland: sometimes called the "master" gland of the endocrine system because it controls the functions of many of the other endocrine glands

Placebo: an inactive preparation prescribed more for the mental relief of the patient than for its actual effect on a disorder or to compare results in a study

Plant-based: consisting primarily or entirely of food (such as vegetables, fruits, nuts, oils, and beans) derived from plants

Polycystic Ovarian Syndrome (PCOS): a group of symptoms that affects the ovaries and ovulation

Pregnant: process of growing a new life inside the female uterus

Prejudice: a negative opinion or feeling about someone or something based on stereotypes or insufficient knowledge

Preservative: a substance used to protect materials from decay

Progesterone: a significant hormone in the reproductive system responsible for pregnancy preparation

Prostaglandins: hormone-like substances that regulate many processes in the body

Receptors: proteins that bind to specific molecules and trigger responses in cells or organs

Recycle: to process (something, such as liquid body waste, glass, or cans) in order to regain material for human use

Reflex: involuntary and nearly instant response to a stimulus

Relaxer: chemical used to treat hair chemically in order to loosen or flatten curls

Reserves: a supply not needed for immediate use but available if required

Reusable: capable of being used again or repeatedly

Saccharin: an artificial sweetener added to foods and beverages

Sacred: highly valued and important

Somatic: of the body, often used to describe various therapies that include physical movements

SOS: an internationally recognized signal of distress

Stagnation: a state or condition marked by lack of flow, movement, or development

Stroke: medical condition in which low blood flow to the brain results in cell damage

Sustainable: something that can last or continue without using up resources or causing environmental damage

Tampon: internal menstrual product designed to absorb menstrual blood and vaginal secretions

Thyroid: a gland that makes and stores hormones that help regulate the body

Trans fats: a type of unsaturated fat that occurs in foods

Treasure Trail: term referring to a line of hair extending from pubic hair up to the navel or belly button

Vaginismus: involuntary tensing of the vagina

Vegan: a strict vegetarian who consumes no food (such as meat, eggs, or dairy) nor uses products from animals

Vegetarian: a person who does not eat meat

Vital sign: critical medical measurements that indicate the status of the body's health

Yeast infections: fungal overgrowth that can cause inflammation, discharge and intense itchiness of the vagina

ACKNOWLEDGMENTS

"Whoever has not thanked people has not thanked God."
– Prophet Muhammad (peace and blessings be upon him)

This book is literally an answer to my prayer, and I learned the power of prayer from my mother. Thank you, Mom, for instilling faith in me from an early age and loving me through the unexpected paths that God has taken me.

Thank you, Daddy, for your love, support, and trust in my judgment.

To my stepparents: Neville and Jo— thank you for loving me as your own.

My brothers: Daawood, Marlon, Brandon, and Neil, I love you all dearly.

Grandma Chin, consider this book your 95th birthday gift. Thank you for your patience with my many questions and curiosities.

To my family-in-love: Mama Carrie, Papa Tommy, Poppi, Ma Linda, and Grandma Jeannie Mae- what an honor to be called daughter and granddaughter by you.

Auntie Brenda- it is said that your maternal aunt is like your mom. Thanks for being a 'second mom' to me.

Aunt Toukei- thank you for the books, letters, and heartfelt conversations. I love you.

Aunt MeMe- thanks for being 'second mom' to my best friend and loving on all of us.

To my sweet nieces and nephews, may you and your children benefit from this book.

To Brooke Benoit, thank you for seeing the worth in my writing before I did. Thank you for believing in this book and being my favorite editor, always.

Thank you, Sisters Na'ima B. Robert, Hend Hegazi, Tumkeen, and Zainab Mir for coaching me through to bring this book to completion.

My gifted illustrator, Sumaya Asvat- thank you for lending your light and inspired art to my words.

My dream formatter, Reyhana Ismail— so glad we finally got to work together.

My beta readers, Elizabeth, Erryn, Ambata, and Mahdiyyah— your early feedback was formative. Thank you!

My esteemed reviewers and contributors: Dr. Laurena, Dr. Emily, Dr. Nicole, Angelica, and Kris— your feedback and support have been invaluable.

To my teacher and comrade, Keli Garza— thank you for your persistence in bringing steaming (back) to all parts of the world. Your support brought this book to fruition. Let the revolution begin!

To my steam sister and muse, Sabrina Elizabeth— it is an honor to know and love you.

To my best friend, Moni- thank you for being such a steadfast sister and loving my family as your own.

To my starseeds, Zahraa, Idris, and Muhammad— three of the greatest blessings in my life after faith. I have grown so much through mothering you all. I have been molded by the unique light each of you bring to the world. Keep shining!

To my husband, life partner, and soulmate Talib. Thank you for keeping your word and supporting my dreams. Your love has given me both roots and wings. No matter where we are, I am always home when I am with you.

DIVE DEEPER

REAL TALK: WHEN PERIODS FEEL UNBEARABLE

At the end of Chapter 3, I mentioned that there are several menstrual conditions that can be extremely challenging for teens, namely PMDD, endometriosis, and menorrhagia. Here is critical information you should know about each condition and what to do if you suspect that you or someone you know might have them.

Premenstrual Dysphoric Disorder AKA PMDD

The major shift of hormones after ovulation can be so overwhelming for some that it brings on symptoms like anxiety, depression, and thoughts of taking one's life. This severe form of PMS is a condition known as PMDD (Premenstrual Dysphoric Disorder), which affects 1 in 20 women. Unfortunately, there isn't nearly enough research to understand why this happens, but some connect its cause to a genetic issue that makes it difficult for women to process hormones and handle stress. PMDD is not like other mental health challenges because the symptoms begin after ovulation and end when the period begins. By tracking when you have particular symptoms and feelings, you can see if your hormones are affecting your mental health.

If your PMDD symptoms include old blood that is brown or black, practices that increase circulation to your uterus will be a priority. Drinking warming teas like ginger, motherwort, or dong quai root can help increase blood flow to your womb, along with womb massage, castor oil packs, and womb steaming. See Chapter 4 for details.

Endometriosis

This is another difficult condition that can be extremely hard to diagnose but equally as hard to ignore. Endometriosis is when tissue similar to what normally grows inside your womb or uterus is growing in other parts of your body. Like uterine tissue, the misplaced tissue responds in the same way and can bleed and shed in different parts of the body. The misplaced tissue can create intense pain and tension when menstruating or when having bowel movements. Severe nausea, constipation, diarrhea, and bloating can occur as well.

To confirm if you have endometriosis, a small camera needs to be inserted into the abdomen to look for misplaced tissue outside of the uterus. It often takes many years for doctors to confirm this condition. The exact cause of endometriosis is not well-understood, but treatment often includes a high-fiber diet with many anti-inflammatory and magnesium-rich foods. Much like with PMDD, womb massage, castor oil packs, and womb steaming can be supportive tools for softening and releasing the misplaced tissue associated with endometriosis. See Chapter 4 for details.

Menorrhagia

Prolonged and abnormally heavy menstrual bleeding is known as menorrhagia. If you're changing period products every hour or need to double up on pads, use overnight pads throughout the day, or use both tampons and pads at the same time, this would be considered menorrhagia. As estrogen makes our uterine lining grow, extra amounts of estrogen can be a cause of excessive bleeding. Therefore, progesterone, which helps to stop the growth of our uterine lining and keep it in place, can help slow down the bleeding.

In medical settings, progesterone or high doses of pain medication might be prescribed, and, in some cases, they might slow down bleeding, though not consistently. If cases like this persist without improvement, it is not uncommon for young women to be advised to consider removing their uterus (hysterectomy) if they don't plan to have children. This suggestion often comes with the assumption that a uterus is only useful for having and growing babies.

Frighteningly, this idea resembles a once-held belief that the uterus causes "hysteria" in women (hence the term hysterectomy). But thankfully, we now know that our wombs are valuable and significantly impact our other body systems. When removed, the body goes through significant hormonal changes that can be just as, if not more, disruptive as the condition that it was intended to relieve.

For alternatives to treating heavy bleeding, we can turn to our original menstrual health experts: traditional midwives. Presently, midwives are seen as birth attendants who can independently support a woman in birth. However, in the past, lay midwives were also herbalists and community-based practitioners who cared for women throughout all stages of their lives. Much like heavy vaginal bleeding in birth, heavy menstrual bleeding can be treated similarly with bed rest and drinking herbs that discourage bleeding, such as shepherd's purse, yarrow, lady's mantle, guava leaves, or mugwort.

If your period flow has exceeded four consecutive days and heavy bleeding persists in spite of the above recommendations, one of the most effective health care practitioners in this case might be an acupuncturist or Traditional Chinese Medicine (TCM) practitioner. TCM is an incredibly comprehensive and well-documented system of health care practices that date back to more than 2000 years ago.

Acupuncturists have time-tested herbal formulas and treatments to slow down or stop bleeding. They are most popularly known for needling—inserting tiny sterile needles at specific points on the body.

ANCIENT WISDOM FOR MODERN TIMES, INTERVIEW WITH ACUPUNCTURIST DR. EMILY SIY

Peaceful Periods: What is an acupuncturist?

Dr. Emily Siy: An acupuncturist is a healthcare provider who treats people based on East Asian medical systems. They primarily use the modality of acupuncture, which is the insertion of thin, sterile needles at specific points in the body, in order to balance the flow of *qi* (or life force) and the circulation of channels (or pathways of energy) and internal organs. Not every acupuncturist is trained in herbal medicine, so if you are seeking consultation in herbal medicine, it is important to ask.

Peaceful Periods: What are treatment options for teens struggling with challenging period issues like menorrhagia, premenstrual dysphoric disorder (PMDD), endometriosis, etc.?

Dr. Emily Siy: Having challenging periods in your teens can be frustrating. East Asian Medicine looks at you as a unique individual. Even though you might have been diagnosed by your doctor with PMDD, endometriosis, or menorrhagia, East Asian Medicine takes into account that there is a unique way these conditions show up in your body. This is why seeking care from East Asian Medicine might give you a better understanding of what is going on in your body. Acupuncture and herbal medicine will be the primary treatment options for challenging periods, but East Asian Medicine is a comprehensive system, and it also includes massage, movement, and meditative practices, as well as nutrition and food therapy.

It is suggested to seek an acupuncturist who is well-trained in menstrual cycle balancing and herbal medicine to help you. Addressing your menstrual cycle imbalances holistically as a teen gives you the opportunity to have more easeful periods in the future.

Peaceful Periods: How do we find an acupuncturist?

Dr. Emily Siy: The best way to find an acupuncturist is by asking your friends and family if they have had acupuncture and know someone they trust who they can recommend to you. You can also seek out acupuncture and herbal pharmacy businesses in your local Chinatowns, Koreatowns, or other Asian communities. Another option is to search for your local acupuncture state organization websites, local acupuncture school, or the national board's website (NCCAOM.org) for their directories of practitioners.

Peaceful Periods: What can we expect during a visit?

Dr. Emily Siy: On your first acupuncture visit, your acupuncturist will look at your tongue and feel your pulse. These are the most common diagnostic tools that acupuncturists use. This will give them some information on how your body deals with fluids, your blood circulation, the health of your digestion, and other organs. The acupuncture itself is nothing to worry about. Acupuncture needles are much thinner than the needles you might have experienced when you've been given a shot or have had blood taken from you. In fact, you can fit anywhere between 8-20 acupuncture needles in a standard injection needle. When an acupuncture needle is first inserted, it can feel prickly, pinchy, or like a mosquito bite.

This feeling dissipates, and it will start to feel more comfortable. Some of the common sensations you can experience are: a dull ache, tingling or static sensation, a quick muscle twitch, heaviness, throbbing, warmth, or coolness. Sometimes you don't feel anything at all. All of these are normal to feel, and sensations can change or come and go as you rest with the acupuncture. Most treatments can last anywhere between 20-45 minutes, depending on what the acupuncturist decides. It is common to feel sleepy, meditative, or very relaxed during and after treatment. Plan to take it easy afterward and make sure you stay hydrated. Some people can feel lightheaded after acupuncture, so it is important to have eaten something before going to treatments so that you are not on an empty stomach. When you get up after treatment, do so slowly to prevent being lightheaded.

NCT JUST HOT AIR, INTERVIEW WITH PERISTEAM HYDROTHERAPIST, KELI GARZA

Peaceful Periods: What is a vaginal steaming facilitator?

Keli Garza: A vaginal, or peristeam, facilitator is a person who specializes in using pelvic steam as a wellness treatment. Steam facilitators offer mobile steam service for individual care at someone's home, have a steam studio at an office, or have a spa where steaming is used as a spa treatment. Sometimes steam facilitators also organize group steam circles or pamper parties. Some steam facilitators also offer virtual consultations where they help someone get set up steaming at home and mail them herbs and other supplies.

Peristeam Hydrotherapists are steam facilitators who have done an intense course of study about women's health issues. They have specific steam protocols for menarche preparation, fertility preparation, labor preparation, postpartum recovery, perimenopause, and postmenopause. In short, they help with all different menstrual life stages.

They are also great support anytime there are any menstrual cycle imbalances or negative period side effects. Peristeam Hydrotherapists believe that painful symptoms and side effects are signs of cycle imbalances. They analyze which imbalances a person's cycle is displaying and create tailored steam plans to target the imbalance by varying the herbs, duration, setup, and schedule based on the user's needs. Some of the menstrual cycle imbalances Peristeam Hydrotherapists might read in the cycle include uterine stagnation, uterine fatigue, dampness, blood deficiency, dryness, excess heat, and weak digestion, which all disrupt menstrual health in various different ways.

Peaceful Periods: How can someone find a vaginal steaming or peristeam facilitator?

Keli Garza: Steaming is a common practice among traditional birthworkers, midwives, medicine women, and herbalists. It's a good practice to start by asking around to find out if there are any traditional steam practitioners in your family or community. To find a certified steam facilitator, check out the Steam Practitioner Directory located at steamychick.com where over a thousand certified practitioners are listed. If there are none in your area, you can set up a virtual appointment. For complicated menstrual issues - like PMDD (Premenstrual Dysphoric Disorder), PCOS (Polycystic Ovarian Syndrome), endometriosis, heavy bleeding, fibroids, infections, and others - it is recommended to book an online consultation with a Peristeam Hydrotherapist.

Peaceful Periods: What does a steam session feel like?

Keli Garza: It feels really nice and relaxing, like a hot bath or shower. Steaming should never be too hot or uncomfortable. It is believed that steaming increases the circulation to the uterus and entire pelvic area, which helps it to perform its functions optimally. Thousands of steam users around the world have shared numerous benefits that they receive. If you'd like to read more individual steam stories, go to steamychick.com and check out the pelvic steam testimonial database.

Peaceful Periods: How often should someone steam?

Keli Garza: Steaming is recommended before and after the period or weekly as a preventative practice. It's best to steam for only 10 minutes and to make sure that you are using herbs best suited for your unique menstrual cycle pattern. If you're not sure, you can use water alone until you have a chance to work with a steam practitioner who can make sure you have herbs unique to your needs.

SIMPLE AND SWEET, INTERVIEW WITH HOMEOPATH MICHELLE PICKERING

Peaceful Periods: What is homeopathy and how does it work?

Michelle Pickering: Homeopathy is based on the principle that the natural state of the body is one of health. As a system of medicine, it aims to assist the natural tendency of the body to gently heal itself by providing a remedy that acts in a similar way to the ailments you are suffering from. This is where the principle of "like cures like" comes from.

Because everyone experiences illness differently, two people with the same ailment may receive two different remedies. In this way, homeopathy is considered individual medicine. Homeopathic remedies stimulate the immune system to assist the body in healing. Therefore, gentle restoration of health and well-being is the aim of homeopathic treatment.

Peaceful Periods: What risks should new users be aware of?

Michelle Pickering: Homeopathic remedies are made by diluting and succussing (vigorously shaking) a substance until there is a miniscule amount of the original material left. A substance is only included as a homeopathic remedy after first being given to healthy people to discover the effects it causes. Your homeopath knows all the outcomes a remedy can produce and will be able to help you navigate any symptoms that arise.

The dose of the homeopathic remedy you receive is very small, and no injurious or harmful side-effects or after-effects should result from using homeopathy. Nonetheless, if you have known allergies to a substance, be sure to discuss this with your homeopath so they are aware and can use the information as a guide in choosing the right remedy for you.

Peaceful Periods: How do we find a homeopathic practitioner?

Michelle Pickering: Most people looking for a homeopathic practitioner these days usually do an internet search, and that's fine. Make sure your practitioner is a graduate from a reputable homeopathic or naturopathic school, investigate their credentials, and ask if they have taken the Certified Classical Homeopath (CCH) exam, which is an examination that determines the extent of their knowledge. Have a conversation and ask lots of questions about their background and what ailments they have treated in the past.

If you need a professional organization to assist in recommending a homeopath in your area, contact the North American Society of Homeopaths (NASH) for help.

RESOURCE HUB

HOMEOPATHIC REMEDY CHART BY JILL GIESINGER

For homeopathic remedies to be effective, they need to match your symptom profile as closely as possible. Before selecting a remedy, read through all the symptoms to see which matches your symptoms best.

Homeopathic Remedy	Period Symptoms
Belladonna	• very painful cramps in the lower back, lower belly, and legs • cutting pains from hip to hip
Calc Carb (Calcarea Carbonica)	• cramps feel like you're being stabbed • labor-like pains (intense cramps that take your breath away) in the back and abdomen before and during period
Caulophyllum	• violent cramps that come and go with little flow • spasmodic intense pains • needle-like sharp pains in cervix
Chamomilla	• labor-like pains (intense cramps that take your breath away), urging to pee • pain is intolerable, wants it taken away NOW
Cimicifuga (Cimicifuga Racemosa)	• crampy pains can shoot down the legs • pain can feel like an electric shock
Cocculus (Cocculus Indicus)	• bloated abdomen with intense cramping • may feel seasick (nauseous, unwell and queasy)
Colocynthis	• sharp, cutting pains • bends forward and holds belly in pain
Cyclamen	• Labor-like pains (intense cramps that take your breath away) that radiate from lower back to the pubic area
Kali Carb (Kalium Carbonicum)	• intense pains during the period that are felt in the lower abdomen, hips, and especially the back • pressure or pushing back into something helps

Homeopathic Remedy	Period Symptoms
Lachesis (Lachesis Mutus)	• the less flow there is, the more intense the pain is • very severe cramps on the first day of the period
Mag Phos (Magnesium Phosphoricum)	• the first choice for menstrual cramps • cramps and pains that are better from heat and pressure
Nux Vomica	• intense pain in the sacrum which urges to move the bowels
Pulsatilla (Pulsatilla Pratensis)	• labor-like (intense cramps that take your breath away) pains, must bend forward • may vomit from the pain • feeling emotional, like you want to cry for any reason
Sabina	• the flow comes in waves along with labor-like (intense cramps that take your breath away) pains • intense pains are better from laying on back with limbs extended out
Sepia (Sepia Officinalis)	• pain during the period with not much flow • there is a heavy, pushing down feeling in the pelvis and vagina • feelings of wanting to be left alone and not disturbed by friends, even close friends • slight feelings of depression during menses
Sulphur	• uterine pains running from groins to back • can have a bearing down feeling in vagina like things will fall out
Viburnum (Viburnum Opulus)	• severe pain wraps from back to lower abdomen • cramping pains shoot down thighs

Note: Homeopathic remedies are prepared according to different dilutions. A 30C dilution is easy to find and effective for most uses, unless advised otherwise by a homeopathic practitioner.

SEASONAL SELF-CARE REFERENCE CHART

MENSTRUAL PHASE/ WINTER SEASON

When: Begins and ends with your period flow

What to do: Focus on rest, warming foods and drinks, and iron-rich, slow-cooked foods

Superpower: Intuition, making important decisions, and spatial reasoning (your internal GPS)

Herbal Allies: Hibiscus, ginger, cinnamon and chamomile

PRE-OVULATORY PHASE/ SPRING SEASON

When: Between the end of the period and before a new egg is released (ovulation)

What to do: Try new activities, eat fermented foods (like yogurt, sauerkraut or kimchi, injera, etc.), and steamed foods

Superpower: Learning new information, imagining big possibilities, and relating to others

Herbal Allies: Nettle and moringa

OVULATORY PHASE/ SUMMER SEASON

When: The 3-4 day window before and after an egg is released from an ovary

What to do: Get physically active and enjoy raw foods like salads and smoothies

Superpower: Stellar speaking skills, glowing skin, and a strong desire to be social

Herbal Allies: Dandelion and turmeric

LUTEAL PHASE/ AUTUMN SEASON

When: From after ovulation until the period starts

What to do: Increase your calories, set boundaries around your time and energy, and eat blood sugar-stabilizing foods like roasted root veggies, whole grains, and beans.

Superpower: Completing tasks, organizing, and analyzing

Herbal Allies: Holy basil and ashwagandha

EMOTIONAL RELEASE TECHNIQUE BY DR. NICOLE MONTEIRO

The Emotional Release Technique is a powerful tool that can help individuals achieve a healthier and more balanced relationship with their emotions. This technique involves six simple steps that can be easily incorporated into your wellness routine.

Emotions are an important part of our inner world and how we relate to others. But many of us respond to our intense emotions by either suppressing them or recklessly letting them spill out.

Step #1 Acknowledge your emotions
This means taking the time to identify what you are feeling and accepting it without judgment.

Step #2 Write out your emotions
Writing out your emotions can help you to process them more effectively and gain a deeper understanding of what is causing them.

Step #3 Shake it off
This involves physically shaking your body to release any tension or negative energy that is held in the body.

Step #4 Wash it away
This involves taking a bath or shower to calm you and symbolizes allowing the emotions to move on. This can be a powerful way to let go of negative energy and create space for more positive thoughts and emotions.

Step #5 Breathe deeply
This involves taking slow, deep breaths to help calm your mind and body - reducing stress and anxiety, and promoting a sense of relaxation and well-being.

Step #6 Release your emotions
This involves letting go of any negative thoughts or emotions and allowing yourself to feel a sense of peace and calm.

Overall, the Emotional Release Technique is a powerful tool that can help individuals achieve greater emotional balance and well-being. By following these six simple steps, you can learn to acknowledge, process, and release your emotions in a healthy and effective way.

LINKS AND FREEBIES

Practitioner Directory

Keli Garza: www.steamychick.com

Jill Giesinger: www.herhomeopathy.ca

Kris González: www.thewayofyin.com

Angelica Lindsey-Ali: www.villageauntie.com

Dr. Nicole Monteiro: www.drnicolemonteiro.com

Michelle Pickering: www.zurimedicine.com

Dr. Emily Siy: www.emilygraceacupuncture.com

Dr. Laurena L. White: www.laurenawhite.com

Free Downloadable Cycle-Syncing Journal and Charting Sheets: www.peaceful-periods.com

REFERENCES

Queen Afua (2001). Sacred Woman: A Guide to Healing the Feminine Body, Mind, and Spirit. Random House Publishing Group.

Baulkman, J. (2016, March 6). All That Multitasking Uses Up Brain Power; Making Women Need More Sleep Than Men. Medical Daily. https://www.medicaldaily.com/women-need-more-sleep-multitasking-brain-power-378045

Blake, C. (2021, November 23). Suicidal Thoughts and Low Iman: How PMDD Could Be Affecting Your Faith and Mental Health. Amaliah. https://www.amaliah.com/post/63556/feeling-suicidal-struggling-to-pray-before-period-pmdd

Burton, N. (2019, July 2). A Study Reveals How Many Women Get *Clinically* Bad Period Pain. Bustle. https://www.bustle.com/p/how-many-women-have-painful-periods-a-new-study-says-its-more-typical-than-youd-think-18164022

Environmental Working Group. (2023, June 2). Learn how Skin Deep ® works. https://www.ewg.org/skindeep/learn_more/about/

Goldhill, O. (2016, February 15). Period pain can be "almost as bad as a heart attack." Why aren't we researching how to treat it? Quartz. https://qz.com/611774/period-pain-can-be-as-bad-as-a-heart-attack-so-why-arent-we-researching-how-to-treat-it

Guttmacher Institute. (2011, November). Beyond Birth Control: The Overlooked Benefits of Oral Contraceptive Pills https://www.guttmacher.org/sites/default/files/report_pdf/beyond-birth-control.pdf

Hendricks-Jack, L. (2019). The Fifth Vital Sign. Fertility Friday Publishing, Inc.

Herlrich-Forster, C., Monecke, S., Spiousas, I., Hovestadt, T., Mitteser, O., & Wehr, T.A. (2021, January 17). Women temporarily synchronize their menstrual cycles with the luminance and gravimetric cycles of the Moon. Science. https://www.science.org/doi/10.1126/sciadv.abe1358

Jardim, N. (2020). Fix Your Period: Six Weeks to Banish Bloating, Conquer Cramps, Manage Moodiness, and Ignite Lasting Hormone Balance. HarperCollins Publishers.

Karchmer, K. (2019). Seeing Red: The One Book Every Woman Needs to Read. Period. S&S/Simon Element.

Kent, T. L. (2011). Wild Feminine: Finding Power, Spirit & Joy in the Female Body. Atria Books/Beyond Words.

Pope, A., & Wurlitzer, S. H. (2017). Wild Power: Discover the Magic of Your Menstrual Cycle and Awaken the Feminine Path to Power. Hay House.

Popova, M. (2013, July 17). Sleep and the Teenage Brain. The Marginalian. https://www.themarginalian.org/2013/07/17/sleep-and-the-teenage-brain/

Smith, M. T. (2020). Your Moontime Magic: A Girl's Guide to Getting Your Period and Loving Your Body. New World Library.

Steamy Chick Institute. (2023, June 10) Cycle Types. https://steamychick.institute/cycle-types/

Vitti, A. (2021). In the Flo: Unlock Your Hormonal Advantage and Revolutionize Your Life. HarperOne.

Vitti, A. (2014). Woman Code: Perfect Your Cycle, Amplify Your Fertility, Supercharge Your Sex Drive, and Become a Power Source. HarperOne.

Walsh, E. (2016, November 1). Dopamine and the Teenage Brain. Spark and Stitch Institute. https://sparkandstitchinstitute.com/dopamine-and-the-teenage-brain/

Walters, M. (2021, September 1). Is There Really a Connection Between Your Menstrual Cycle and the Moon? Healthline. https://www.healthline.com/health/womens-health/menstrual-cycle-and-the-moon

Weschler, T. (2006). Cycle Savvy: The Smart Teen's Guide to the Mysteries of Her Body. William Morrow Paperbacks.

Weschler, T. (2015). Taking Charge of Your Fertility, 20th Anniversary Edition: The Definitive Guide to Natural Birth Control, Pregnancy Achievement, and Reproductive Health. William Morrow Paperbacks.

INDEX

A

Abdomen and Abdominal 30, 39-40, 57, 72, 108, 120, 130-131
Absent periods 54, 55, 91
Acne 12, 29, 30, 66, 77
Acupuncture 5, 9, 24, 58, 121-123
Addiction 80
Affirmation 39, 40
Aggression 70
Alkaline 61
Allergies 53, 126
Amino acid 82
Ammonia 61
Anemia 55
Antibacterial 63
Antibiotics 66, 79, 102, 107
Antidepressant 102, 107
Anti-inflammatory 29-30, 69, 107, 120
Antipsychotic 102, 107
Anus 19, 62, 108
Anxiety 55, 119, 134
Appetite 50, 68
Art 34, 73, 109, 116
Aspartame 79, 107
Aspirin 29
Athletes 82, 101
Autumn See phases
Ayurvedic 24, 58

B

Bacteria 61, 63, 67, 69, 79, 107
Basal body temperature 50, 57, 91, 92, 95, 107, 110
Beans See food
Biohacking 94
Birth 9, 12, 29–32, 97, 102, 108, 120, 137, 138
Birthworkers 125
Bladder 72
Bleach 98, 99
Bloated/bloating 21, 22, 29, 31, 48, 57, 58, 66, 78, 91, 108, 119, 130, 137
Blue light 14, 75, 108
Bone 33, 41, 66, 111, 112
Brain 20, 25, 26, 33, 44, 45, 48, 65, 71, 74, 75, 77, 80, 87, 108, 114
Breakfast 17, 66–68
Breakouts 91
Breast 9, 26, 33, 35, 48, 78
Butter See food

C

Caffeine 69, 70, 80, 81, 84, 88, 108, 109
Cancer 31, 66, 72, 108
Canola oil 36
Carbohydrates/carbs 49, 102, 103
Cardio 88, 89
Castor oil 40, 42, 119, 120
Cervical and cervix 19, 50, 52, 60–62, 64, 91, 93, 105, 108, 110, 130
Chart and Charting 5, 28, 49, 50, 59, 91–93, 95, 130, 132, 136
Chemical 13, 25, 62, 70, 72, 77, 81, 82, 98, 99, 108, 109, 110–12, 113
Circadian 44, 88, 108, 111
Circulation 30, 36, 39, 41, 53, 54, 82, 94, 119, 122, 123, 125

139

Clot 22, 31, 35, 36, 40, 52, 54, 89, 94, 108
Constipation 4, 33, 56, 57, 78, 109, 119
Cramp 4, 12, 16, 18, 20, 22, 24, 26, 29, 30, 33–36, 39, 46, 52, 54, 66, 73, 83, 89, 95, 97, 99, 130, 131, 137
Craving 4, 22, 35, 46, 67, 77, 82
Creativity 20, 74, 94, 97
Cry 131

D

Dance 14, 41, 74, 81, 89, 94, 102
Deficiency 54, 55, 97, 109, 124
Delayed 14, 29, 101, 109
Deodorants 72
Depression 31, 119, 131
Detergent 13, 62
Diabetes 31, 66, 109
Diarrhea 34, 57, 119
Digestion 55, 57, 58, 66, 123, 124
Discharge 55, 56, 60, 62, 63, 91, 109, 114
Dysmenorrhea 29
Dysphoric 119, 122, 125

E

Elimination 15, 57, 77, 109
Emotional 5, 7, 22, 25, 53, 71, 103, 108, 111, 131, 134-135
Emotional release technique 5, 71, 134-135
Endocrine and endocrinology 9, 13, 25, 109, 113
Endometriosis 9, 109, 119, 120, 122, 125
Energy 18, 25, 44, 46–50, 53, 67–70, 80, 81, 84, 87–89, 94, 101, 112, 122, 133, 134
Estrogen 26, 47, 48, 60, 61, 72, 78, 80, 82, 83, 94, 102, 110, 120
Exercise 14, 48, 71, 72, 74, 87–90, 101, 102

F

Factory-farmed 13, 17, 69, 79, 110
Fat 29, 36, 67, 68, 78-80, 82, 89, 101-103, 114
Ferment 9, 13, 69, 132
Fertile 22, 27, 50, 60, 61, 102, 108
Fertility 9, 93, 110, 124, 137–39
Fertilization 26, 34, 60, 110
Food
   Almond 35, 67
   Amaranth 67
   Barley 70
   Beans 13, 18, 46, 48, 49, 53, 66-68, 82, 83, 102, 113, 133
   Beef 17, 84
   Beets 50, 53
   Boba 56
   Buckwheat 50, 70
   Butter 36, 39, 63, 67, 68, 82, 83, 104
   Cacao 35, 46
   Cashew 81
   Cheese 13, 49, 63, 68, 79, 82, 83
   Chickpea 67, 70
   Chocolate 35, 46, 72
   Cider 37
   Cocoa 35, 46
   Coconut 36, 39, 63, 67, 69, 79
   Dates 22, 67, 68
   Energy drinks 69, 70, 81, 88
   Garlic 81, 82
   Ghee 36, 82
   Grains See grains
   Hazelnuts 35
   Honey 67, 69, 83
   Hummus 18
   Injera 132
   Junk food See junk food

Kale 18, 81
Kidney 29, 31, 56, 109
Kimchi 132
Lemon 13, 79, 82, 84
Lentil 67, 82
Lime 79, 82
Maple syrup 52, 67, 69, 82
Margarine 78
Masala 18
Meat See meat
Miso 80
Natto 80
Nuts See nuts
Okra 56
Olive 36, 39, 68, 72, 82
Pad Thai 18
Paratha 67
Peanut 69, 82
Pistachios 68
Quinoa 70, 82
Rye 70
Sauerkraut 132
Sausages 67
Sesame 82
Shellfish 102
Soy 61, 69, 80
Tallow 82
Tapioca 56
Tea See tea
Tempeh 80
Watercress 56
Yogurt 67, 79, 132
Footwear 73
Foul-smelling 56, 62, 63
Fried 36, 77, 78

G

Gas 57, 58, 89, 108
Genes and genetic 80, 101, 110, 119
Gluten 55, 61, 69, 70, 80
GMOs 80
Grain 13, 48, 50, 66-70, 82, 133

H

Heart-womb 14
Hemp seeds 67
Herbs
   Ashwagandha 53, 82, 133
   Astragalus 53
   Basil 81, 82, 133
   Burdock 70
   Calendula 57
   Cinnamon 67, 83, 132
   Comfrey 57
   Dandelion 70, 82, 132
   Dong quai 119
   Garlic 81, 82
   Ginger 30, 46, 82, 83, 105, 119, 132
   Ginseng 53
   Hibiscus 56, 83, 132
   Kukicha 70
   Lavender 63
   Maca 70
   Marjoram 81
   Mint 37, 47, 57, 63
   Moringa 82, 132
   Motherwort 119
   Mugwort 53, 121
   Nettle 47, 82, 132
   Oregano 81
   Peppermint 63
   Raspberry Leaf 53

Rosemary 63

  Shatavari 56

  Shepherd's purse 53, 121

  Thyme 81

  Turmeric 30, 82, 132

  Yarrow 53, 121

Hip 26, 35, 39, 40–42, 73, 105, 130

Homeopath 5, 36, 126, 127, 130, 131

Hormonal and hormone 9, 10, 12, 13, 15, 20-22, 24-31, 45-46, 48-50, 60, 65-70, 72, 74, 78-82, 84-85, 87-89, 91, 94-95, 97, 101-102, 109-114, 119-120, 138

Hydrating and hydration 56, 66, 79, 81

Hydrotherapist and hydrotherapy 5, 24, 39, 52, 58, 112, 124, 125

Hygiene 7, 55, 62–64

Hysteria 120

I

Ibuprofen 29

Imbalances

  Blood deficiency 54, 55, 124

  Dampness 55, 124

  Dryness 56, 57, 99, 124

  Excess heat 56, 124

  Stagnation 14, 53, 73, 124

  Uterine fatigue 53, 124

  Weak digestion 57-58

Immune and immunity 67, 107, 126

Inflammation and inflammatory 29, 36, 68-69, 85, 111, 114

Infradian 45, 88, 111

Insulin 65, 66, 109, 111

Intuition 45, 46, 71, 97, 111, 132

Iodine 102

Iron 46, 53, 55, 82, 102, 132

Irritable and irritability 21, 44, 67, 78, 111

Irritation 63, 99, 111

Itch and itchiness 56, 63, 99, 114

J

Junk food 64, 65, 77

L

Labia 62

Luteal 48, 49, 57, 82, 89, 93, 133

M

Magnesium 35, 46, 102, 120, 131

Make-up 72

Massage 39–42, 119, 120, 122

Meat 18, 46, 49, 53, 66, 79, 80, 83, 84, 114

Meat-free 17, 84

Medication 29, 31, 60, 97, 102, 107, 120

Menarche 6, 15, 45, 101, 112, 124

Menopausal and menopause 9, 15, 45, 57, 112

Menstrual dysfunction 9, 105

Mental health 2, 119, 137

  Antidepressant 102, 107

  Antipsychotic 102, 107

  Anxiety 55, 119, 134

  Depression 31, 119, 131

  Hysteria 120

  Overwhelm 13, 49, 55, 87, 97, 119

  Stress 15, 22, 27, 41, 49, 58, 61, 65–72, 74, 76, 80, 83, 85, 87, 89, 90, 101–3, 108, 110, 119, 134 See mood

Metabolism 47, 48, 50, 79, 112

Migraines 91

Mono-sodium glutamate (MSG) 77

Mood 4, 25, 31, 33, 45, 48, 55, 66, 74, 78, 97, 137

Mucus 16, 35, 50, 52, 55, 56, 60–64, 91, 93, 105, 108–10

Muscle 30, 33, 35, 41, 68, 73, 74, 82, 83, 89, 123

N

Naproxen 29

Nausea 31, 34, 57, 119

Nervous system 87, 108

Night sweats 56, 57

NSAIDs 29, 32

Nuts 35, 36, 49, 68, 69, 82, 102, 113

Nutrition and nutritional 13, 22, 53, 55, 79, 81, 84, 101-102, 122

O

Odor 9, 56, 60-63, 77, 99

Oil 13, 36, 39, 40, 42, 63, 78, 81, 113, 119, 120

Organs 2, 25, 27, 33, 58, 65, 68, 101, 111, 113, 122, 123

Ovaries and ovary 10, 19, 25, 27, 31, 47, 65, 112, 113, 125, 132

Overwhelm 13, 49, 55, 87, 97, 119

Ovulate, ovulation and ovulatory 24-27, 29, 30, 47-50, 52, 55, 60-61, 65, 66, 68, 74-75, 82, 87, 89, 93-95, 101-103, 109, 112, 113, 119, 132, 133

P

Pad 14-16, 18, 20, 24, 26, 30, 35, 40, 58, 98, 99, 104, 120

Pain 2, 9, 10, 12, 14, 16-18, 20, 22-24, 26, 29–33, 35, 40-42, 52, 54, 66, 69, 84, 89, 97, 99, 105, 109, 112, 119, 120, 124, 130, 131, 137

Panties and panty 15, 56, 58, 62, 63, 98, 99

PCOS See polycystic ovarian syndrome

Pelvic and pelvis 14, 36, 41, 73, 112, 124, 125, 131

Perimenopause 124

Perineum 19, 62, 112

Phases
  Luteal/Autumn 48, 49, 57, 82, 89, 93, 133
  Menstrual/Winter 46, 95, 132
  Ovulatory/Summer 47, 48, 82, 94, 132
  Pre-Ovulatory/Spring 47, 132

Plastic 13, 73, 78, 98–100

Plastic-free 15, 98

Polycystic Ovarian Syndrome (PCOS) 9, 112, 113, 125

Pregnancy and pregnant 22, 25-26, 30, 78, 84, 110, 113, 138

Premenstrual 21, 52, 119, 122, 125

Premenstrual Dysphoric Disorder (PMDD) 119, 120, 122, 125, 137

Premenstrual Syndrome (PMS) 10, 12, 22, 42, 52, 119

Progesterone 26, 27, 47–50, 55, 57, 58, 61, 78, 82, 94, 102, 109, 113, 120

R

Rash 56, 57

Relaxer 72, 113

Reproductive 7, 9, 10, 105, 110, 113, 138

S

Sauna 36-38, 102

Scent 9, 13, 61–64, 99

Seasons See phases

Selenium 102

Self-esteem 6, 22, 73, 100

Shapewear 41

Spatial 47, 132

Sperm 60, 61, 110

Spiritual 17, 34, 45, 84, 111

Spring 47, 51, 79, 132

Steam 36–39, 42, 54, 56, 63, 81, 105, 112, 116, 119, 120, 124, 125, 132

Stevia 69

Stomach ulcers 29, 31

Stress 15, 22, 26, 27, 33, 41, 49, 58, 61, 65, 67-71, 74, 75, 80, 82, 85, 87, 89, 90, 101–3, 108, 110, 119, 134

Sucralose 79

Sugar 15, 46, 49, 55, 61, 63, 65-69, 75, 77-79, 81-82, 89, 104

Summer 45–48, 51, 132

Sunflower oil 36

Sweat 37, 57, 74, 88-89, 97

Sweet 36, 50, 67, 69, 78-79, 81-83

Sweetener 67

Syrup 52, 67, 69, 79, 82

T

Tampon 20, 35, 58, 98-99, 106, 114, 120

Tea 30, 34–37, 39, 46, 56-57, 69, 80, 83, 105

Testosterone 27, 47, 82

Toxins 77, 88

Track 21, 44, 50, 52, 58, 59, 72, 75, 91, 95, 110, 119

Traditional Chinese Medicine (TCM) 52, 121

U

Urethra 19, 39, 62

Uterine

cramping 18, 33-35, 39, 52, 54, 89, 94, 99, 130-131

fatigue 53, 124

lining 26, 34, 35, 109, 112, 120

Uterus-strengthening 53

V

Vaginal

Discharge 55, 56, 60, 62, 63, 91, 109, 114

Discomfort 63, 64

Infection 56

Irritation 63

Vegan 17, 18, 80, 84, 114

Vegetarian 13, 17, 18, 66, 79, 84, 114

Vinegar 13, 37, 81

Vulva 19, 37, 38, 50, 62–64, 98–100

W

Waist 16, 41, 72 See shapewear

Walk 10, 16, 47, 73, 74, 88

Warmth 33, 35, 36, 39, 41, 42, 54, 56, 57, 94, 123

Weight gain 31

Weight loss 72, 101

Womb massage 39, 42, 119, 120

Womb steaming 36, 42, 54, 56, 105, 119, 120

Wrap 16, 21, 38, 40, 41, 49, 99, 105, 131

Y

Yeast infections 31, 114

Yoga 88

AUTHOR BIOGRAPHY

Chantal Blake is a Holistic Menstrual Health Educator and Writer, with a professional background in Nursing, Environmental Engineering, and Peristeam Hydrotherapy. She weaves the fields of medicine, environmentalism, and holistic self-care into fascinating and practical instruction for women of all ages.

Since 2019, Chantal has helped hundreds of women experience healthier periods and greater allyship with their female design through consultations, courses, and private coaching. Her work continues to reach an ever-growing audience through published articles, podcast interviews, and speaking engagements. As a world traveler and serial expat, Chantal has learned how to communicate her heartfelt desire to see women flourishing in their female design across cultures, contexts, and languages. And as a wife and mother of three, she is extremely passionate about nurturing a legacy of women who love their periods, honor their wombs, and protect their fertility for generations to come.

You can follow Chantal's work at www.honoredwomb.com and on Instagram: @honoredwomb

Milton Keynes UK
Ingram Content Group UK Ltd.
UKHW050754310124
436998UK00010B/95